ROYCE'S SOCIAL INFINITE

Royce's Social Infinite

The Community of Interpretation

BY

JOHN E. SMITH

With a new Preface by the Author

ARCHON BOOKS
1969

SBN: 208 00729 6
Library of Congress Catalog Card Number: 69-13630
Printed in the United States of America

CONTENTS

It was somewhat monstrous, and in this wilderness with nobody to talk with about it, I have not the least idea whether it is true or not. . .

—Royce to William James, 1879, Concerning a Philosophical Theory he was then teaching at California.

PREFACE

A study of the literature reflecting the philosophical influence of Josiah Royce reveals that at least three very important and valuable parts of his thought have, up to the present time, not been sufficiently treated. These are: the theory of the community of interpretation, the debt to Charles Peirce's thought, particularly his logic, and finally the interpretation of Christianity. Each of these has consequences worthy of note both in philosophy and in related fields of thought. Besides the fact that the community theme furnishes a vantage point from which Royce's entire thought may be surveyed and understood, the theory of the community of interpretation has interesting implications for philosophy which have yet to be explored. Royce's debt to Peirce is not only important historically, but it provides as well an illustration of the important use to which the results of certain logical analyses may be put, and shows that although modern logic may often seem to be barren where synthetic philosophy is concerned it is not so necessarily. In some respects, as the body of this study will show, Royce's interpretation of Christianity is the most significant of all. Unfortunately it has often been believed that Royce only offered some idealistic substitute for traditional Christianity, as Santayana thought, and this, it may be added, has contributed to the neglect of his religious thought. That he offered no such substitute a reading of *The Problem of Christianity* will demonstrate. His view of Christianity has a peculiar significance at present, for, while he should not be called "neo-orthodox" in one of the senses of that rather vague term, he did try to steer a middle course between naive Fundamentalism on the one hand and that liberalism which hoped to confine itself to the "religion of the historical Jesus," on the other. It would certainly not be incorrect to say that Royce's Christianity is in accord with the main drift of certain leading Protestant thinkers at present.

Although my main purpose has been to set forth Royce's

thought and its background with as much clarity as possible, I have sought now and then to remove the discussion from the purely historical context either by criticizing a particular doctrine or by breaking a small lance for Royce's view where I believed it defensible. I can only hope that this practice has not destroyed the continuity of the main discussion.

As for intellectual and spiritual indebtedness one is always primarily in the debt of one's teachers, whether through their persons or through their writings or both. I cannot name here all those, at present my colleagues both in Columbia University and Union Theological Seminary, upon whom I have depended for guidance both philosophically and theologically, but nevertheless I acknowledge the debt and I am grateful to them. In particular I am grateful for the invaluable assistance of my wife in many ways; she has well exemplified the spirit of loyalty.

J. E. S.

BARNARD COLLEGE, COLUMBIA UNIVERSITY
New York, April, 1949.

PREFACE TO THE 1969 EDITION

Nearly two decades have passed since this book first appeared. During that time significant progress has been made both in the interpretation and critical discussion of Royce's thought and in the reprinting of his works. In 1955 the Eastern Division of the American Philosophical Association scheduled as part of its annual meeting, a Symposium devoted exclusively to Royce's philosophy; in 1967 an entire issue of the *Revue Internationale de Philosophie* was given over to articles dealing with theories and concepts basic to Royce's many-sided interpretation of things. In the period between 1950 and the present time, moreover, important books and articles have been written aimed at elucidating Royce's ideas and at showing the importance of his philosophical contribution. In order to paint the background against which *Royce's Social Infinite* makes its reappearance, I shall give a brief resume of the philosophical work that has been done in recent years and of the works that have been reprinted.

J. Harry Cotton's study, *Royce on the Human Self*, which appeared in 1954, is important not only for its penetration into Royce's ideas but also for its scope. No other work brings as much of Royce's thought within the compass of a single study. The theory of the individual self runs from one end of Royce's thought to the other, and Cotton uses that theme in order to give a coherent account of Royce's idealism. Especially significant are Cotton's interpretation of the connection between idealism and voluntarism, and his pointing up of the relation between the interpretation of logic as the science of order and the idea of the self-representative system which is exemplified in the community.

Also of importance is the English translation of four articles on Royce's metaphysics written by Gabriel Marcel and originally published in *La Revue de Metaphysique et de Morale* in the years 1918–19. The translation by Virginia and Gordon Ringer appeared in 1956. Unfortunately, I discovered Marcel's original articles too late for use in writing the present volume. I still regard this fact as a misfortune because Marcel's analysis takes positive and perceptive account of Royce's theory of interpretation and the logic of the community. Marcel nicely appreciates the differences between Royce's voluntarism and the pragmatic position, as well as the similarities between the two. Moreover, he sees clearly the extent to which the Absolute Knower of Royce's earlier thought develops into the Interpreter of the later community doctrine. Most significant of all, Marcel grasped the affinities with existentialism in Royce's theory of the self as a purpose or plan.

Royce's ethics, expressed in his *Philosophy of Loyalty* and other writings, was curiously neglected until the fine study by Peter Fuss, *The Moral Philosophy of Josiah Royce*, which appeared in 1965. With exceeding clarity and precision, Fuss shows the development of Royce's thought on the ethical problem, together with the psychological (especially the theory of imitation) and epistemological considerations that underlie his view. Fuss gives not only a critical reconstruction of Royce's loyalty ethic relating it to some current positions, but he candidly faces the puzzle familiar to every student of Royce—exactly how is the later theory of interpretation related to Royce's initial philosophy of the Absolute?

It is interesting to note that scholars in other countries are paying attention to Royce's ideas. This interest is well illustrated in a monograph by K. T. Humbach, *Das Verhältnis von Einzelperson und Gemeinschaft nach Josiah Royce* published in Heidelberg in 1962. This book represents the first comprehensive excursion into Royce's political philosophy and attempts to show the connections between the many human communities delineated in Royce's writings. Though more expository than critical, the work is valuable.

Those interested in Royce and in the contemporary significance of his ideas have recently been aided by the reprinting of works that have been unavailable for many years. Within the past fifteen years, *California, The Religious Aspect of Philosophy, The Spirit of Modern Philosophy, The World and the Individual*, the *Lectures on Modern Idealism* and *Studies of Good and Evil* have all been reprinted. In addition, Daniel Robinson has collected a number of Royce's papers dealing primarily with logical topics under the title, *Logical Essays,* and Royce's contribution, "The Principles of Logic," to Windelband's *Encyclopädie,* has recently been made available in a paperback edition. Finally, the most difficult of all Royce's books to obtain, *The Problem of Christianity,* has been reset and reissued by the University of Chicago Press with an introduction in which I attempt to interpret for the contemporary reader Royce's final excursion into the philosophy of religion.

As *The Problem of Christianity* makes clear, Royce was determined to express the nature of a community in as exact terms as possible; he had made considerable progress in this direction by means of the theory of signs and interpretation. In an unpublished letter, probably written in 1913, to Professor Warner Fite, Royce referred to what he described as "the *most* elementary logical problem involved in my theory of the 'community'." That problem, as subsequent paragraphs make clear, concerns the formal properties of the relation between an individual and an assemblage. Royce explains that he did not consider the problem in strictly logical terms in *The Problem of Christianity* because of the popular make-up of the audience to which the original lectures were addressed. Royce's ensuing explanation is of the utmost importance for the theory of the community not only because of the light it throws on the nature of the latter, but also in furnishing an excellent illustration of Royce's belief in the value of formal logic for metaphysical analysis.

It will be helpful to anticipate the result at which Royce aims, so that the connection between the formal considerations to follow and the concrete religious and ethical interests of the community will not be lost. Two features of actual community were special objects of Royce's interest; each concerns contrast of relations. First, there is the difference between the relation of the individual member to the community and that of the community to the individual member, and, second, there is the difference between the relation of each member to each other, and the relation of each member to the community. By means of Peano's conception of the "E=relation," or the relation of belonging to or being a member of an assemblage,

Royce sought to clarify these relations and especially to avoid confusion between (a) the love which a member has for the *community*, (b) the love the community has for the member, and (c)
the love which an individual has for the *other* members of the
community.

After noting some logical properties of the E=relation, Royce
singled out its *non-reflexivity* and *asymmetry* as fundamental. By the
non-reflexivity of the E=relation is meant that no entity stands in
that relation to itself. The individual X may belong to the collection
a ("X εa"), but that individual cannot stand in the E=relation to
itself. Royce was at this time familiar with Russell's claim that supposing the E=relation to be reflexive would lead to contradictions.
The use Royce was to make of the non-reflexive character of the
E=relation will be made clear after a brief account of the *second*
property, that of asymmetry. If an individual X belongs to a collection a, symbolized as "X ε a", then the converse of that relation,
symbolized as "a ε X" is always false, because the collection does
not belong to the individual as the individual belongs to the collection. Applying this point to the philosophy of the community, Royce
notes that if I am a member of a community, however I may stand
related to it, it does not stand related to me in the same way. I
love my community, and my community loves me, but the two
"loves" are different and neither is to be understood in accordance
with the model of *lover* and *beloved* when these are two *individuals*.
My love for the community is the love of an individual for a certain
spiritual collection; the love which the community has for me is
on another level, since it is *not* the love of an individual for another
individual, but the love of a community for an individual. Moreover,
the relation of an individual to his community—the E=relation—
differs from any relation holding between individual members, for
no two individuals stand in the E=relation to each other. The relations of each individual to his community are all profoundly affected
by the basic E=relation, but the relations between the individual
members all differ from that basic relationship, since it never holds
between two individuals.

From Royce's standpoint, the upshot of the discussion, and it is crucial for his entire philosophy of community, is that you cannot understand what community is and means if you take as a model for your analysis the relation between one individual and another. For on that model, the E=relation is absent, and the community does not come into view. Stated otherwise, Royce was rejecting the nominalist approach to community which starts with "this individual" passes to "that individual," conjoining them with "and," a conjunction which is a purely external relation, and never confronts the E=relation which is the essential basis of the community.

The point previously made about the non-reflexivity of the E= relation, assumes major importance in Royce's account of the religious community, where we see that it is precisely the individual's relation to that community which overcomes his moral burden and places him in a right relation with God. Since no individual has the E=relation to himself, no individual can save himself. Since, moreover, the E=relation does not obtain between two individuals, but only between an individual and a community, no one is in the religious sense saved, merely by becoming related to any other individual. It is at this point that the novelty of Royce's insight becomes most apparent; the consciousness which one individual has of another individual is radically different from the consciousness which an individual has of a community. All forms of social life take us beyond the immediate relation of individual to individual and on to the relations of all individuals to the spirtual unities or communities to which they belong. This insight is at the root of Royce's reinterpretation of the Christian understanding of life in terms of the Beloved Community.

John E. Smith

New Haven, Conn.
December, 1968

ACKNOWLEDGMENTS

I wish to thank the following for permission to quote from copyrighted material:

Mr. Stephen Royce of Crystal Falls, Michigan, for Josiah Royce's works: *The Conception of God*, 1898; *The World and the Individual*, 2 volumes, 1899-1902; *The Problem of Christianity*, 2 volumes, 1913; *War and Insurance*, 1914; and *The Hope of the Great Community*, 1916.

Harvard University Press, Cambridge, Mass., for *Fugitive Essays* (1925), edited, with an introduction, by J. Loewenberg; and *Collected Papers of Charles Sanders Peirce*, 6 volumes (1931-1935), edited by Charles Hartshorne and Paul Weiss.

The Trustees of Lake Forest University, Lake Forest, Illinois, for, Josiah Royce, *The Sources of Religious Insight*, 1912.

The Macmillan Company, New York, for Josiah Royce's works: *The Philosophy of Loyalty*, 1908; and *William James and other Essays*, 1911.

J.E.S.

ROYCE'S SOCIAL INFINITE

CHAPTER ONE

THE IDEA OF INFINITE COMMUNITY

Josiah Royce's most mature philosophical idea, that of the community of interpretation, provided a resolution of the most important problems upon which he had thought and written throughout his philosophical career. Royce said as much himself in the autobiographical remarks made at a dinner given in his honor in 1915: "I strongly feel that my deepest motives and problems have centered about the idea of the Community, although this idea has only come gradually to my clear consciousness."[1]

Professor Loewenberg, in a discussion of the development of Royce's thought, recognizes the central importance of the community idea and calls attention to its application to just those practical and theoretical problems which this study seeks to emphasize. He says,

> In the idea of the Community, as he understood it, modern thought has received one of its richest philosophic conceptions. With its aid Royce sought to interpret the deepest issues of metaphysics, the profoundest problems of knowledge, the ultimate questions of religion. And so focal is it in his ethics that, from his point of view, the whole moral task of humanity finds in terms of the community articulate expression.[2]

Royce's four main subjects of inquiry, two theoretical, metaphysics and epistemology, and two practical, ethics and religion, are related to his doctrine of the community of interpretation as an infinite system. The idea of the Great Community and the theory of social insurance (see Chapter VI) occupied the thoughts

---

[1] These words based on notes taken at the dinner may be found in many places. Rand has reproduced them in *Papers in Honor of Josiah Royce*, pp. 279-86. They appear again in *The Hope of the Great Community*, pp. 122-36. The particular sentence in the text is quoted by Loewenberg in his Introduction to *Fugitive Essays*, pp. 36-7.

[2] *Fugitive Essays*, Editor's Introduction, p. 37.

of his last years,[3] and illustrate perhaps more vividly than any others the seriousness with which he took the idea of the triadic structure of interpretation and the possibility of its application to the most immediate and pressing problems which mankind is ever called upon to face.

Royce, following the lead of Peirce in his theory that the community ultimately supplies the ground for the validity of logical principles, maintained that no knowledge of the kind called scientific is ever possible apart from the community and the ideal of truth to which the members of that community are devoted. Royce was willing, to a certain degree, to follow the formulations of pragmatism and consequently he spoke of ideas as "leadings" and "working hypotheses" both of which are dependent on empirical data and which lead to or direct inquiry to further data. This familiar view of the perceptual and the conceptual elements in scientific investigation is correct as far as it goes, said Royce, but what it neglects is the further processes of thought and observation by means of which scientific discoveries cease to be confined to their original locus and assume that status of universality characteristic of genuine scientific knowledge. This transition from the "private" to the "public" requires many acts of confirmation both in the field directly concerned and in related fields. That is, no discovery formulated as an assertion and based upon evidence can be admitted to the body of knowledge constituting a science until it has been subjected to the scrutiny and further analysis of others working in the same domain and capable of reproducing such conditions as may be necessary for testing the truth of the assertion in question. According to Royce, this process presupposes, and indeed takes place within, the *scientific community*. "The individual," so Royce put it, "has made his discovery; but it is a scientific discovery only in case it can become, through further confirmation, the property and the experience of the community of scientific observers."[4]

The further analysis and observation by which what purports

[3] *War and Insurance* appeared in 1914, and *The Hope of the Great Community* in November, 1916, two months after Royce's death.

[4] *The Problem of Christianity*, II, 231.

to be knowledge is tested requires a process of interpretation and, hence, what Royce called a community of interpretation. An investigator who seeks to confirm or refute certain proposed assertions based on discoveries already made, is involved in a process of interpretation having a triadic structure, because he seeks to compare (a) the available evidence with (b) the assertions which he is attempting to test (signs), and the result of this process will be (c) a further interpretation standing in need of the same critical analysis from which it has resulted, and so on. This chain of interpretations is, for Royce, the very life of the scientific community, and the truth concerning the world consists in the whole body of such interpretations which in the course of time become the common property of this community of interpretation. The world of common objects, presupposed in daily experience, as well as the world of scientific knowledge rests on a community of interpretation precisely because no common-sense observer ever directly experiences a *common object*. Such an object is the result of interpretation,[5] for each observer can only verify assertions by reference to his own percepts alone and never to those of any one else. Common objects therefore are the result of interpretation and as such presuppose the community of interpretation which is infinite in character.

Truth, on this view, is the ideal goal of the scientific[6] community and it is the cause to which the members of that community are devoted. The purpose of this community of interpretation is expressed once for all in saying that it seeks truth wherever truth may be found, and the will of this community, according to Royce, comes to be fully expressed through the unending chain of interpretations to which the search for truth gives rise. Truth is a reality only in so far as the goal of this community is a reality, and the whole company of seekers for truth have worked in the belief, explicit or implicit, that such a goal is real, although in its

[5] This may be a highly complicated process as it is in scientific research or the almost unnoticed interpretation of commonsense in its belief in a world of common objects. See *The Problem of Christianity*, II, 240ff.

[6] This term must be taken in a broad sense and one not confined, as is so often the case, to the physical sciences.

fulness it can never be experienced by any member or collection
of members constituting the scientific community.

The central task of metaphysics, for Royce, was the clarification and justification of the community of interpretation in all
its forms. In turning to metaphysics in the search for a warrant
for believing in the reality of such communities, Royce was led
to develop a very interesting and significant thesis: philosophy
is neither the work of conception nor of perception (intuition)
alone, but an enterprise of interpretation. "Philosophers," he said,

> have actually devoted themselves in the main, neither to perceiving the
> world, nor to spinning webs of conceptual theory, but to interpreting
> the meaning of civilizations which they have represented, and to attempt-
> ing the interpretation of whatever minds in the universe, human or
> divine, they believed to be real.[7]

For the elucidation of this thesis Royce selected the philosophies
of Plato and Bergson as obvious representatives of the two contrasting approaches; Plato for his emphasis upon the purely
intelligible aspect of existence and Bergson for his emphasis upon
the intuitive grasp of reality from within. What Royce was
seeking to show is that actually each philosopher, in dealing
with the inescapable antithesis between *appearance* and *reality*,
the *private* and the *public*, the *false* and the *true*, offers some *interpretation* of this contrast as the substance of his philosophy, and
also that the assertion "the real or the true is found through
concepts or through intuition" is not itself the result of either
conception or perception, but is an interpretation. Royce considered it impossible to view the real world in simple monistic
fashion[8] as if all ideas could be blended into a single idea, like
Spinoza's concept of substance, or as if all of reality could be
grasped in some one act of immediate vision or intuition. For the
idea of a real world comes to us only as a result of the problematic
situation, that is, the contrast between appearance and reality,
with all its conflicts, antitheses and problems, which we all face.
"*By the 'real world' we mean*," he said, "*simply the 'true interpre-*

[7] *Ibid.*, II, 255.
[8] Since this may be a surprise to some, see *ibid.*, II, pp. 260ff.

tation' of this our problematic situation.'' [9] In so far as this is a correct view of our situation, the "real world" is an explicit interpretation of the contrast between the idea of present experience with all its fragmentariness and the idea of the goal of experience. No single idea, such as a monistic philosophy might propose, will suffice to interpret this contrast because the fact that such a contrast exists and that it calls for an interpretation which is itself a sign, shows that no single idea we now possess interprets it fully. What is required for a full interpretation is the community, the true infinite system. The philosopher, nevertheless, is one who seeks some special interpretation of the antithesis between the world of fleeting experience and the stable, common, public, true, or real world. Royce wrote:

> Every special definition of reality takes the form of offering such a solution. Whether a philosopher calls himself realist or idealist, monist or pluralist, theist or materialist, empiricist or rationalist, his philosophy, whenever he states it, takes the form of saying: "The true, the genuine interpretation of the antithesis is such and such."[10]

The interpretation offered is real only if the community of interpretation serving as its basis is real, and it is true only if that community attains its goal. Royce argued that if the real world is the community of interpretation constituted by the foregoing antithesis together with the mediating idea or interpreter, the success of this community is intimately bound up with the reality of both the antithesis and the interpreter. "*Unless*," he concluded, "*both the interpreter and the community are real, there is no real world.*"[11] As a proper corrective to the many possible misinterpretations of this view of reality, the following paragraphs containing Royce's own estimate of his position are of singular importance:

> After the foregoing discussion of the nature and the processes of interpretation, we are now secure from any accusation that, from this point of view, the real world is anything merely static, or is a mere

[9] *Ibid.*, pp. 264f.

[10] *Ibid.*, II, 268f.

[11] *Ibid.*, II, 270.

idea within the mind of a finite self, or is an Absolute that is divorced from its appearances, or is any merely conceptual reality, or is "out of time," or is a "block universe," or is an object of a merely mystical intuition.

Interpretation, as we have seen in our general discussion of the cognitive process in question, demands that at least an infinite series of distinct individual acts of interpretation shall take place, unless the interpretation which is in question is arbitrarily interrupted. If, then, the real world contains the Community of Interpretation just characterized, this community of interpretation expresses its life in an infinite series of individual interpretations, each of which occupies its own place in a perfectly real order of time.[12]

To go on from the theoretical to the practical subjects of the inquiry, it is now necessary to indicate briefly the relation of the community idea to ethics and religion. Royce himself has told us that *The Philosophy of Loyalty* represents the first formulation of his ethical opinions to follow his discussion of practical problems in *The Religious Aspect of Philosophy*.[13] This later formulation centers about the idea of loyalty and devotion to a cause uniting many men together in a community. At the time of *The Philosophy of Loyalty*, however, Royce had not yet given the clear formulation of the nature and structure of the community that he finally came to give in the analysis of the community of interpretation in the second volume of *The Problem of Christianity*.[14] By this time he had made Peirce's idea of signs having three correlates his own, and he had extended Peirce's theory to his doctrine of interpretation and the community of minds following from this. Hence when Royce spoke of loyalty and community in his later works, the community to which he referred can be defined with a precision that was not possible at the time when the loyalty theme first came to his mind.

    [12] *Ibid.*, II, 270f. That a community of interpretation as above defined satisfies the conditions of an actual concrete infinite is clear. See the "Supplementary Essay" in Vol. I of *The World and the Individual*.

    [13] *The Philosophy of Loyalty*, p. ix.

    [14] See Royce's own remarks on the development of the loyalty theme in *War and Insurance*, Note III, pp. 85-6, and Note I, p. 83. See also the article by W. E. Hocking on Royce in *Encyclopedia of the Social Sciences*, XIII, 451b ff.

The Kantian background of his views on ethics led him to consider duty of the greatest importance.[15] Royce, however, always sought the possibility of some concrete realization of tasks and duties, and for this reason he did not confine his interests to the purely formal aspect of ethics which so attracted Kant. Loyalty is the highest good for Royce, and it always requires, besides the individual's conscious choice of a cause, some *practical* deed having concrete consequences for human society. This stress on the importance of practical expression must not be overlooked in any attempt to understand Royce's position, for it is never absent in any of his ethical writings and it even figures in his most abstract principle: Be loyal to loyalty. Although this appears at first sight to be the most hazy of commands and perhaps worthy only of an idealist, Royce was careful to point out that in so far as every individual, wherever he be, stands in some social relationship, his duty is to manifest loyalty by concrete deeds *in his particular situation*, and that in this way he indirectly contributes to the extension of loyalty to the whole of mankind.

The community here, as everywhere in Royce's thought, is at the very center. Loyalty is always devotion to a cause, and a cause is what unites the company of those devoted to it into a community. Actually all the communities of interpretation of which he wrote in his many works are based on loyalty (and this is really another name for Royce's understanding of the Pauline *caritas*), because each community requires for its continued existence the sustained loyalty of its members to the goal for which it exists. Thus the scientific community, for example, requires that its members be loyal to the cause of truth as the goal toward which the scientific community strives, and the beloved community requires that its members be devoted to God as the supreme goal envisaged by the religious community. The value of community in all its instances is twofold; by showing the individual a supreme value which introduces some harmony among his conflicting inclinations it helps him toward self-realization, and by inter-

[15] Note, for example, Royce's preoccupation in his last years with the "*duties of Americans*" in relation to the war and the hoped-for peace. See also *The Sources of Religious Insight*, pp. 170ff.

preting all its members to all its other members through a common past and a common future it brings about a unity and harmony among persons such as would not otherwise be possible.

It is not necessary at this juncture to speak at length concerning the relation between the idea of community and Royce's philosophy of religion, since this will be treated most fully in the main discussion. It is enough to mention here the direction which his thought took on this head. The reconciling function of community is nowhere better illustrated in Royce's thought than in the instance of religion. In *The Sources of Religious Insight*[16] he suggested that genuine religion should accomplish the individual need for salvation or reconciliation, provide for some visible sign of salvation through union with the brethren, contain a coherent view of truth, and satisfy the "aim of the will to conform itself to the laws of the master of life with whom we need to be united."[17]

The beloved community, as will be clear in the sequel, accomplishes all of these tasks and it does so through the one spirit which pervades the whole and continually reminds the members, through many acts of interpretation, that they are all members one of another. The spirit or interpreter of the beloved community makes salvation possible and does so in corporate terms; the interpreter is the spirit leading into all truth; and finally the interpreter not only directs the individual will to God by revealing the lord of life, but he so interprets one member to another that each is enabled thereby to manifest that love of neighbor which is of the essence of the divine kingdom. When Jesus said, "For where two or three are gathered together in my name, there am I in the midst of them,"[18] he was really speaking of the beloved community which Royce described so well. According to Royce's doctrine, whenever two are gathered together in the name of the Christ, there are three, for then the interpreter binds them together in that love or charity which is divine.

[16] *Op. cit.*, p. 166.

[17] *Loc. cit.*

[18] Matthew 18:20.

CHAPTER TWO

THE BACKGROUND: PEIRCE'S THOUGHT AND THE PHILOSOPHY OF LOYALTY

From the outset, Royce was concerned with the problem of the concrete or actual infinite, and that problem had, for him, both a practical and a theoretical aspect. In its theoretical aspect the problem of the actual infinite presented itself to Royce as a problem both in metaphysics and in the theory of knowledge. On its practical side it appeared as a problem in ethics and in religion. Royce was equally interested in both sides because from the very beginning he sought not only the "religious aspect of philosophy" but also the philosophical foundation of religion. He believed that on the one hand the truth concerning the real world must involve the genuine goal of all human striving as well as that salvation which is the hope of religion, and that on the other, the genuine good for man and the true and ultimate redemption in religion must be rooted in some defensible view both as to the nature of truth and of the real world. It is the central aim of this study to show that in Royce's view of the community of interpretation as infinite system, the true form of the actual infinite, set forth most fully in *The Problem of Christianity*, is to be found a solution to his central problem in all its aspects. For in the doctrine of the community we find at once what was for Royce the correct view of the nature of truth, the true interpretation of the absolute, the final goal of all striving, and the salvation which is the aim of religion. In the discussion which follows the theoretical aspect of Royce's thought will be considered in the chapter "Community of Interpretation as Infinite System" and the practical aspect will be dealt with in the chapters "The Beloved Community" and "The Great Community." The relations between these two aspects will also be made clear.

In those sections of his first book, *The Religious Aspect of*

11

Philosophy, which are best known (and indeed often taken as the whole of Royce's position), he dealt with the problem of the absolute as it had been formulated in the attempts of the post-Kantian idealists to restore metaphysics after the severe criticism of Kant. Royce showed dissatisfaction with all *purely* practical or voluntaristic solutions involving a complete neglect of any attempt to provide a theoretical or rational warrant for the reality of the infinite. He sought to pass beyond the contingency of moral striving and the element of uncertainty and relativity necessarily connected with the world of "mere" ideals.[1] In short, he sought the Absolute, not as a mere ideal, but as an actuality. In this attempted elimination of all doubt he adopted a method which, although by no means original with him, he used with acuteness and with somewhat surprising results. Royce proposed an analysis of doubt itself and of the presuppositions of the doubter, which he carried through in the ingenious section "The Possibility of Error" in *The Religious Aspect of Philosophy*. This analysis is so well known that there is no need to repeat it; however the conclusion reached is noteworthy as is Royce's own account of the steps by which he came to it. Absolute truth, he argued there, must be found in the conditions which make error possible. Earlier in the work he had hinted that doubt contained within itself the resolution of doubt, and in the course of the discussion it becomes clear that the dialectical extraction of absolute truth from doubt and error is that to which he referred.

One part of the discussion of the possibility of error in this first book foreshadows the later community theory, namely, the well-known section concerning an imaginary conversation between John and Thomas, introduced for the analysis of errors in regard to other minds. Some elucidation of this may be valuable. When two persons, John and Thomas (to use Royce's illustration), attempt to hold a conversation there are actually six persons present: the real John and Thomas, Thomas' and John's ideas of themselves and each of their ideas of each other. Royce pro-

---

[1] See *The Religious Aspect of Philosophy*, pp. 436ff. This is also clearly stated in *The Sources of Religious Insight*, pp. 221-223. *Cf.* Hegel in *The Philosophy of Right* and F. H. Bradley in *Ethical Studies*.

posed to deal only with four which shall be here designated as follows: real John (J), real Thomas (T), John's idea of Thomas (T') and Thomas' idea of John (J'). Neither J nor T is able to be in error about T and J respectively because, as Royce had pointed out previously, an assertion can only be false when it stands in a relation, not to any object, but to its *intended* object, which is such as to render the assertion false.[2] Since neither J nor T can ever intend T and J but only T' and J', because the former are never present in their experience, it is impossible for them to be in error, for error by definition is always about T and J. If, however, a third mind were present containing experiences common to both J and T, he might provide a ground for J and T, and then error would be possible.[3] What is significant here is that the *third* or mediator is precisely what introduces the absolute thought or *is* the absolute thought, but Royce did not pursue the point further since at that stage of the analysis he was concerned only with the criticism of common-sense assumptions, not with a final resolution of his problem.[4] The idea that the absolute thought takes the form of a third or interpretant is of decisive importance in the complete formulation of the community metaphysic, but at this early stage Royce had not yet discovered the idea of mediation through interpretation; rather he was thinking in terms of integration and intuition.

This last point is of the highest importance. Royce's thought exhibits a very definite development in the conception of the Absolute, and since the thesis that in the Absolute thought all ethical, religious, and philosophical problems are solved is central to his view, it is of some moment to be clear about this development. Speaking generally, the all-important change in

[2] See Peirce, *Collected Papers*, V, 329, where it is stated that an assertion can only be judged according to what it asserts. All future references to Peirce's papers are to sections and not pages.

[3] H. W. Schneider is correct in his remark that error is as difficult to achieve as truth on idealist principles (*A History of American Philosophy*, p. 484). It should not be overlooked, however, that the ingenuity of the analysis consists in Royce's having chosen error, whose reality presumably no one would care to deny, as the fact from which to derive the concept of *absolute truth*.

[4] *The Religious Aspect of Philosophy*, p. 411; cf. p. 415 and especially p. 422.

Royce's conception of the Absolute consists in the shift from the idea that the Infinite thought is an all-embracing consciousness apprehending *at a glance* all truth and harmonizing at once all conflicts between the multiplicity of finite wills in existence, to the idea that the Infinite is actual as a well-ordered system (or ultimately, community) having a general triadic form and in- volving a type of cognition called interpretation. This change in Royce's view may be stated, using some terms he himself em- ployed in *The Spirit of Modern Philosophy*, as the supplanting of *appreciation* by *description*. The Absolute of *The Religious Aspect of Philosophy*, of *The Spirit of Modern Philosophy* and of *The Con- ception of God*[5] is a self who knows the totality *totum simul*, that is, immediately and at a glance and without any reference to before and after. However, from *The World and the Individual* (particularly the "Supplementary Essay" at the end of Volume I)[6] on to the final statement in *The Problem of Christianity*, the idea of the Absolute as a well-ordered system or community of inter- pretation and of the importance (even necessity) of mediation, as opposed to appreciation, were uppermost in his mind.

A brief examination of some of Royce's earlier statements concerning the Absolute Self will serve to establish the correct- ness of the foregoing remarks about the development of that conception. In the all-important chapter "The Religious Insight" in *The Religious Aspect of Philosophy*, Royce characterized the Absolute as both the all-embracing unity of thought and the infinite life in which is contained as already real those goods which finite beings seek to attain; the Absolute is both Truth and Good. He said, referring to our finite progress both in the attainment of knowledge and in the embodiment of the good:

But for God this is no real progress. Therefore is it indeed true that the moral insight in us must lead us to aim at progress in goodness, just as, on the other side, the rational element in us leads us to aim at progress in knowledge. But, meanwhile, our moral progress and our

[5] In this work, however, particularly in the supplementary essay, Royce showed signs of his later position. The points he conceded in answer to Howison's criticism support this statement.

[6] See below for some qualification of this statement.

rational progress, mere minor facts happening at a moment, are but insignificant elements in the infinite life in which, as a whole, there is and can be no progress, but only an infinite variety of the forms of the good will and of the higher knowledge.[7]

Royce's emphasis in the above passage is clearly upon the completeness, the wholeness and the finality of the Absolute as such. What is actual for finite beings only under the form of time, that is, as a process in which *before* and *after* are meaningful terms, is real for the Absolute all at once. This applies, as is clear from the foregoing, both to the Absolute as thought and as will, but at this point in his development it was the Absolute as thought that predominated. "That all facts and relations of facts," said Royce, "should appear *in one moment* of insight to the all-knowing thought is our postulate, and, as we have shown, it is no mere postulate, but a necessary and absolute principle of philosophy."[8]

The significant point is the phrase "in one moment," or as Royce expressed the same idea in other places, *totum simul*. The Absolute is here conceived as possessing a consciousness different from that of a finite being precisely because it is a time-spanning consciousness. It possesses at once and presumably intuitively what is only capable of being grasped by a finite consciousness in mediate or discursive fashion. One further passage from Royce's early book will make this more clear:

As my thought at any time, and however engaged, combines several fragmentary thoughts into the unity of *one Conscious moment*, so, we affirm, does the Universal thought combine the thought of all of us into an absolute unity of thought, together with all the objects and all the thoughts about these objects that are, or have been, or will be, or can be in the Universe.[9]

Again the stress is upon the simultaneous grasp of truth by the Absolute in a way which is synoptic and intuitive rather than

[7] *The Religious Aspect of Philosophy*, p. 467.
[8] *Ibid.*, p. 461. (Italics not in original.)
[9] *Ibid.*, pp. 475f. (Italics not in original.)

discursive in character. This is a distinctive feature of Royce's earlier view of the Absolute Self.

In *The Spirit of Modern Philosophy* this same basic emphasis is to be found, and the Absolute Self is said to be possessed of a knowledge which is in some sense not discursive but immediate. Only there the contrast takes the form of the difference between what Royce called the domain of *description* and that of *appreciation*. Royce distinguished, in the lecture entitled "Physical Law and Freedom,"[10] between experiences capable of being communicated through a description employing relational and other concepts which enable us to compare these experiences with others and in this way reach objective or permanent experience, and experiences which are *appreciated* by us in immediacy but not susceptible of descriptive communication. The describable experience is public property precisely because it is reproducible, and also because description makes use of certain forms or categories expressing definite recurrent relations. The appreciated, on the other hand, is that which is not describable in these terms and hence is confined to the individual experiencing subject. The appreciated, one may say, is therefore private. Yet, said Royce, if the world of appreciation is to be regarded as ultimately real, "then the appreciations, it would seem, must not be the appreciations of *merely* temporal and transient beings but of some being that himself does not live in moments, as we mortals on earth do, but that appreciates in eternity, or shares in such an eternal appreciation."[11] In pursuing this theme Royce arrived once again at the view of an Absolute Self possessing a type of consciousness which is synoptic in nature and which grasps as a whole and from within what is only known by finite minds from without, that is, descriptively and hence discursively. Many passages from *The Spirit of Modern Philosophy* might be given to illustrate the view of the time-spanning consciousness which Royce then held, but the following are the most explicit:

    1. We have suggested hypothetically what a "World of Appreciation"

---

[10] See *The Spirit of Modern Philosophy*, pp. 381ff.
[11] *Ibid.*, p. 393.

might be. It would be a world such as the organic Self in his wholeness might have present to him at a glance. . . ."[12]

2. When, namely, I physically describe, that is, explain events by their causes, I first seize upon some one instant of time, some one event, and ask: What *is* the configuration of the world *now*? Having found in a measure this description of one moment of the world, this cross section of the temporal series of events, I ask myself: How did this condition result from the previous state of the world? Descriptively, or contemplatively, then, I study the world *from* one moment to another. But when I view a physical series appreciatively, when I estimate the world, or any part of it, say a kind action, or the inner life of my friend, or a process of evolution, I don't thus dwell on the momentary description or configuration of things, but I, as it were, take in at one glance a whole series of moments.[13]

3. Whatever the true facts about what we call time may be, as they are known to the Self, we are sure that the order of nature, from what we are obliged to call the infinite past to the infinite future, just *because* it does all of it express one law, just *because* it must all be absolutely foreknown, is present in one time-transcending instant to the insight of the Logos. . . . This transcending of a time-series, and estimating it as one whole, is in fact what one might call the soul of the natural order."[14]

4. But the whole temporal order is for the Absolute Self, of whom you are a part, only one way of looking at truth. All eternity is before him at a glance.[15]

In both *The Conception of God* and *The World and the Individual* Royce still maintained the idea that the Absolute Self is to be defined in terms of wholeness, unity and inclusiveness of insight which is immediate or appreciative in character.[16] The *totum simul* aspect of the Absolute is still to be found there, but an important change was taking place. Royce was beginning to stress the ideas of *system* and of *order* as definitive of the Absolute, and mediation was beginning to assume an importance for him which it had not formerly possessed; Royce retained the *totum simul*, although

[12] *Ibid.*, p. 397.
[13] *Ibid.*, p. 424.
[14] *Ibid.*, pp. 430f.
[15] *Ibid.*, pp. 433f.
[16] See, for example, *The Conception of God*, esp. p. 8. Cf. pp. 298ff.; also *The World and the Individual*, I., 568, 580, 582f.

in the form of purpose or will; he tended to accentuate the element of mediation instead of appreciation. When Royce conceived of the Infinite as ordered experience or as system, and when he emphasized mediation at the expense of immediacy, he was on the track which led to the idea of the community of interpretation as infinite system.

The procedure adopted by Royce in arriving at the metaphysical concept of absolute truth illustrates the method which he always followed in his philosophy. He began with an accepted fact and sought to show that its reality necessitates the reality of its conditions, etc., until the analysis finally results in the necessary recognition of the infinite or absolute.[17] In this respect he was justified in calling attention to the empirical character of his philosophy. He maintained the concept of absolute truth as a necessary one, but one which as such is derived from concrete experience. Royce never made the error of supposing that one single fact about the actual world could be derived from such a concept alone, and in this respect he cannot be charged with any attempt to "deduce" the actual world *a priori*.

The path outlined by Royce as the one along which he traveled to the positive conclusions of *The Religious Aspect of Philosophy* is of importance for an understanding of his most cogent reasonings in *The Problem of Christianity*. He accepted the critical philosophy of Kant in opposition to a common-sense standpoint which, according to Royce, assumes that "the whole matter is sure from the outset,"[18] but he was dissatisfied with what he called the postulational view. As Royce understood it, Kant's position with regard to knowledge involved certainty only of the present moment and left past and future with no other guarantee than that of postulates. If this is a true account, Royce maintained, doubt is possible concerning them, and, since doubt involves error, the further question arises: How is error possible? From this beginning in fact and after a careful attempt to show that error is not possible on the assumptions of common sense about the truth of isolated assertions, Royce concluded that

[17] *Cf.* Dewey in *Papers in Honor of Josiah Royce*, p. 26.
[18] *The Religious Aspect of Philosophy*, p. 390.

error is possible only if absolute truth is actual in the form of an absolute thought. At this time he conceived such an all-embracing and inclusive thought after the fashion of a cosmic mind, distinguished from the finite minds by the possession of the characteristic of knowing, as complete and final, what is only fragmentary and provisional for us. Although in the course of his philosophic development[19] Royce never lost his view concerning the insufficiency of a purely voluntaristic solution of the problem of the Absolute and hence the necessity for a *concrete* as distinct from an abstract or ideal universal, he ultimately came to think of it in terms of an infinite *community*.[20] That this aspect of Royce's thought has never been adequately investigated is unfortunate, because the community theory, as will be shown, represents a clear logical analysis of ethical, religious and metaphysical problems, rarely ever treated with anything like the acuteness Royce exhibited in those lectures.[21]

There can be little doubt that Royce's view of the ultimate reality as an infinite community was largely dependent on certain fundamental notions developed in some early essays of Charles Peirce. Royce willingly acknowledged his debt[22] to Peirce, and he was always careful to indicate precisely the points at which

[19] See *Contemporary Idealism in America*, ed. C. Barrett, for the remarks of Professor Palmer on Royce's development: "He was ever changing, ever constant. In this his first book (Palmer refers here to Royce's *Primer of Logical Analysis for the Use of Composition Students*) he treats of a subject on which his thoughts were largely engaged at the time of his death. But how differently the subject was conceived! That was always his mode of progress. He carried his past with him, not dropping conceptions but evolving them continually into richer significance" (pp. 5f.).

[20] See *The Problem of Christianity*, I, xi, where he notes that he is not simply restating the thesis of *The World and the Individual*. It is important to note that Royce's development of his metaphysic in this direction admirably illustrates the general thesis of H. W. Schneider in *A History of American Philosophy* concerning the trend of idealism in America. He says, "The emphasis on mind as objective logical structure has grown at the expense of the Absolute" (p. 492). Royce's development from *The Religious Aspect of Philosophy* to *The Problem of Christianity* is the best possible illustration of this thesis.

[21] *The Problem of Christianity*, delivered as lectures at the Lowell Institute, Boston, and at Manchester College, Oxford.

[22] *Ibid.*, I, xi; II, 114, 116, 117; cf. II, 182-186.

he intended to leave Peirce behind[23] and give a metaphysical generalization for which he alone could be held responsible. Royce regarded Peirce as a logician of the first rank and even took the trouble to offer some slight account of the latter's independent discovery of the doctrine of the "third" or the interpretant, from Peirce's study of logical problems, particularly the logic of relations, rather than from any direct Hegelian influence.[24] The Community metaphysic of Royce, as will be shown more fully later, was the result of a careful study on his part of certain principles of logic held by Peirce as well as the metaphysical generalization of these in the light of certain ethical and religious considerations drawn from his investigations of the spirit of loyalty. The larger context within which the entire metaphysical discussion ultimately takes place is what Royce came to regard as the "problem of Christianity."

A great deal will be said of Peirce's ideas in the course of the discussion, but worthy of some mention at this point are Peirce's idea of the following: (a) the community as that which ultimately guarantees truth and reality, (b) the idea of a sign as determining an interpretant, (c) the idea of comparison, (d) the idea that no intuitive knowledge of the self is possible, and (e) the idea that all self-knowledge is essentially discursive, involving both relations with other selves and the interpretation of certain signs. In the second volume of *The Problem of Christianity*,[25] Royce noted the essays of Charles Peirce to which he was most indebted. A careful study of these early papers together with Peirce's article

[23] *Ibid.*, II, 116 (and other places).

[24] *Loc. cit.* Cf. *The World and the Individual*, I, 526f., where Royce said that his discussion of the infinite as self-representative system is dependent on Dedekind and other mathematicians and not on Hegel.

It may be well to note here that Royce has too often been classified as an "Absolute Idealist" after the pattern of Hegel, and no doubt Royce's failure to have a greater influence on American philosophy is to be traced to this identification. Royce, as his books testify, studied and respected German Idealism and he was indebted to that tradition, but it is important not to overlook the other sources of his thought (Peirce, Dedekind, Schroeder, *et al.*), especially since he was himself anxious to point these out and to anticipate the tendency of his readers to identify his thought prematurely with that of the German philosophers.

[25] *Ibid.*, II, 114.

"Sign" in *Baldwin's Dictionary*[26] throws a great deal of light upon Royce's theory of the community. It also lends considerable and welcome clarity to the whole analysis; for Royce, it must be admitted, was a rhetorical writer and he often leaves one in doubt as to the precise meaning of his more moving phrases.

The papers of Peirce are specifically the following: 1. "On a New List of Categories" (1867), *Collected Papers*, I, 545ff. 2. "Questions Concerning Certain Faculties Claimed for Man" (1868), *Collected Papers*, V, 213ff. 3. "Some Consequences of Four Incapacities" (1868), *Collected Papers*, V, 264ff. 4. "Grounds of Validity of the Laws of Logic," *Collected Papers*, V, 319ff. These papers, supplemented by an important discussion by De Morgan[27] on the theory of the syllogism and the logic of relations, provide the logical framework underlying the most mature statement of the Roycean philosophy.

In the first of the papers listed Peirce offered an analysis of our knowledge of quality through *comparison*. Quality, he held, cannot be known without reference to the relations of (a) being similar to or (b) being in contrast with,[28] and these require that *correlates* be introduced. Comparison, according to Peirce is always a *triadic* relation[29] which requires a mediator. As he stated in another place,[30] illustrations are often more helpful than formal definitions, although these are obviously indispensible. Peirce's illustrations here will serve to make his meaning clear. When two ideas or perceptions are compared, as, for example, the letter p with the letter b, a mediating idea or image is required which represents the *respect* in which they are related. In this instance the mental image representing p when rotated in appropriate fashion, as the likeness of b, is the mediator or third. Peirce offered another illustration, this one from language forms. Upon

---

[26] *Baldwin's Dictionary of Philosophy and Psychology*, II, 527.

[27] De Morgan, "On the Syllogism No. IV and on the Logic of Relations," *Cambridge Philosophical Transactions*, (1866), X, 331-358.

[28] *Collected Papers*, I, 552.

[29] That it is *triadic* is of great importance because Royce criticized all *dyadic* theories on this ground.

[30] *Ibid.*, I, 553.

finding the word *homme* in a French-English dictionary we discover that the word *man* is the equivalent, which means that *man* represents *homme* as standing for the same being which *man* itself stands for. If this is generalized in Peirce's language, a mediating representation represents some relate (*homme*) to be a representation of the same correlate (two-legged creature) which the mediating representation (*man*) itself represents.[31] Peirce called the "third" an interpretant because it functions in precisely the same way as an interpreter functions. An interpreter translates some signs (words and phrases) into other signs (words and phrases) and says, in effect: What I say is what is said by these signs. Represented schematically, interpretation appears as follows:

A. Signs to be interpreted.

B. Interpreter.

C. Interpretation.

B. offers a new set of signs which are addressed to a future interpreter and which are said to represent what A represents. Peirce was aware that he employed the term "representation" in a broad sense, meaning by it the capacity of any sign to relate something to a conception in the mind of the appropriate hearer. The relation between the process of comparison and an interpretant on Peirce's view can be made clear only by reference to the course of knowing the manifold of experience. The confusion characterizing the beginning of inquiry leads, according to him, to an attempt at differentiation within the subject matter, and finally to some unity of knowledge. Comparisons yield knowledge of *quality* and the interpretants or signs, which mediate between what is to be distinguished, provide the unifying concepts of general relations which are the goal of all scientific knowledge. It is important to bear in mind the broad sense in which Peirce and Royce, as will be evident, used the term comparison. The

[31] *Cf.* Peirce's article "Sign" in *Baldwin's Dictionary*. "Anything which determines something else (its interpretant) to refer to an object to which itself refers (its object) in the same way, the interpretant becoming in turn a sign, and so on *ad infinitum*" (p. 527, col. 2).

term is capable of application to situations such as a criminal proceeding in which the prosecution and the defence stand in the relation of opposition, or in religion where the prophet is faced with two or more ideas for which he attempts to give an interpretation.

In the notes[32] to this paper of 1867 which Peirce added at a later time, he mentioned a paper sent him by Augustus De Morgan[33] in which the latter dealt with the problem so central to present logical theory—of providing foundations for the syllogism by using the general category of relation rather than the traditional notion of class inclusion and exclusion. It is not with the entire discussion that one need be concerned, but only with that part of it which, as Peirce himself saw, gives logical support to the idea of an interpretant. De Morgan expressed dissatisfaction with the traditional logical principles of *identity*, *non-contradiction* and *excluded middle*, not because he regarded them as logically unsound, but because of their inadequacy for distinguishing or evolving one truth from another. According to De Morgan's criticism, every transgression of these laws is an invalid inference and every valid inference is not a transgression of these laws, but he denied that everything not a transgression of these laws is a valid inference. De Morgan maintained that all inference can not be obtained through the ordinary syllogism in which the terms of the conclusion must be terms of the premises. If, however, the category of general relation be admitted, including convertible and transitive relations, a theory of the syllogism can be given exhibiting, "in the most general form, the law of thought which connects two notions by their connections with a third."[34] Stating this more formally, De Morgan wrote, "the supreme law of syllogism of three terms, the law which governs every possible case, and to which every variety of expression must be brought before infer-

---

[32] *Collected Papers*, I, 56off.

[33] "On the Syllogism No. IV and on the Logic of Relations," *Cambridge Philosophical Transactions*, X, 331-358.

[34] *Ibid.*, p. 347.

ence can be made, is this: any relation of X to Y compounded with any relation of Y to Z gives a relation of X to Z."[35]

It is important that De Morgan regarded a theory of the syllogism based on the logic of relations as providing the general form of deriving any third or mediating notion (what Peirce called an *interpretant*). According to De Morgan, relation as such is the basic category in all inference. The following paragraph expresses this very clearly:

Any objects of thought brought together by the mind, and thought together in one act of thought, are *in relation*. Should any one deny this by producing two notions of which he defies me to state the relation, I tell him that he has stated it himself: he has made me think the notions in the relation of *alleged impossibility or relation*. [cf. this with Peirce's illustrations offered above]; and he has made his own objection commit suicide. Two thoughts cannot be brought together in thought except by a thought: which last thought contains their relation.[36]

Peirce recognized that here, in the context of a discussion of inference, was a purely formal statement of a third or interpretant. His own comment on this paper of De Morgan's is interesting. After reading it he came to certain conclusions about the various types of predicates, and with respect to predicates having three subjects (interpretants), he said, "These last (though the purely formal, mathematical method of De Morgan does not, as far as I see, warrant this) never express mere brute fact, but always some relation of an intellectual nature, being either constituted by action of a mental kind or implying some general law."[37] As can be seen from the standpoint of Royce's theory there is a steady progression from the *purely formal* presentation of De Morgan through the largely *epistemological* discussion of Peirce to the explicitly *metaphysical* use of the interpretant as it appears in Royce's theory of the real world as the true interpretation.

In the paper entitled "Questions Concerning Certain Faculties Claimed for Man,"[38] Peirce dealt with the problem of intuition

[35] *Ibid.*, p. 338.

[36] *Ibid.*, p. 339.

[37] *Collected Papers*, I, 562.

[38] *Ibid.*, V, 213ff.

in various aspects and raised the question of our capacity for an intuitive knowledge of ourselves. Since Royce made important use of Peirce's conclusion in this matter, some statement of the latter's argument is necessary. Peirce began by denying that we can decide *intuitively*[39] the question whether or no a given cognition refers to its object immediately or is the result of a previous cognition. In support of the denial he maintained a distinction between having an intuition and knowing intuitively that something is an intuition. From this distinction it follows that no logical *distinction* is intuitive because an intuition is always something *had* and not the way of *knowing* something else.[40] Passing on to the specific problem of self-knowledge, Peirce held that knowledge of "I" (not of the "I" which is "pure apperception") is not intuitive, because what we know about ourselves comes through discursive thought based on what others tell us of ourselves. Also, ignorance and error require a self which is fallible, and ignorance and error are discovered only through the acquisition and interpretation of testimony involving mediation. "Testimony," Peirce concluded, "gives the first dawning of self-consciousness."[41] He made the point more secure in his analysis of emotional reaction with the following illustration: Mr. A. directs his anger towards a certain object. That the anger is not literally a character possessed by the object seems clear, but yet some one of its characters has occasioned anger. What Mr. A. is first aware of is "this or that is vile," and only later reflections yield "I am angry." This process of reflection leading to self-knowledge is what Peirce regarded as incompatible with the assertion that Mr. A. knows himself intuitively.[42]

In the paper entitled "Some Consequences of Four Incapaci-

---

[39] Peirce defined intuition as a cognition determined by something out of consciousness and "nearly equal" to a "premise not itself a conclusion" (*Collected Papers*, V, 313).

[40] See Sec. 262 which is crucial on this point. Since cognition of an intuition involves relation, it takes time, that is, is not immediate, and relations are always determined by previous cognitions.

[41] *Ibid.*, V, 233.

[42] Further discussion of the correctness of these analyses will be postponed until the discussion of Royce's use of them for his own purposes.

ties,"[43] Peirce set forth his definition of the real and showed the inseparability of reality and community. In one of the sections in this paper,[44] most important for the understanding of Royce, Peirce argued as follows:

Since at a given moment we possess cognitions, the result of previous inductions, etc., whose antecedent cognitions may be demanded in a process without end, we must finally come to a first, something singular. "This ideal first," said Peirce, "is the particular thing in itself. It does not exist *as such*. That is, there is no such thing which is in-itself in the sense of not being relative to the mind, though things which are relative to the mind doubtless are, apart from that relation."[45] The cognitions at which we ultimately arrive can be divided into (a) cognitions whose objects are real, (b) cognitions whose objects are unreal. The question which now arises is: What do we mean by *real*? The discovery of the problem first comes in the recognition of error and illusion.[46] Illusion is occasioned by a judgment on the part of an isolated individual that some *ens* appearing in him is real, when further analysis, involving others, proves that the *ens* in question appeared *only* to him and has no further reality beyond his consciousness. Illusion or unreality consists in a private individual being a judge in his own case and affirming to be real what further analysis must deny. This implies that the real is what is affirmed and confirmed by the community of investigators in the course of time, for only a community can possess truth about the long run. Peirce expressed this as follows: "Thus the very origin of the conception of reality shows that this conception essentially involves the notion of COMMUNITY, without definite limits, and capable of a definite increase of knowledge."[47]

[43] *Ibid.*, V, 311f.

[44] *Loc. cit.*

[45] *Loc. cit.*

[46] Cf. the argument of Royce in *The Religious Aspect of Philosophy*.

[47] *Collected Papers*, V, 311. This is a crucial section in Peirce and the basic idea is employed in Royce's analysis as a statement of the form in which the absolute or infinite is actual. Cf. also the paragraph from Peirce's review of Berkeley's works in the *North American Review*, 1871, pp. 449-472, a great part of which is reproduced in H. W. Schneider, *A History of American Philosophy*,

Peirce regarded his theory as an essentially realistic one, since whatever phenomenalism is still retained by it is that of the mind of the community and not any particular mind.[48] This, according to Peirce, if it be phenomenalism, is that of Kant and not of Hume. For objective or warranted truth is possible for man, but only as the result of much investigation involving a host of minds. In the long run the community reaches the truth (approximates Kant's *Bewusstsein überhaupt*) with the greatest degree of certainty ever possible for finite minds.

Peirce made one other point in this paper which ultimately bears upon the Roycean metaphysic; the view that man is identical with his thoughts. To be a thinking being man must employ signs as the interpretants of his thoughts, and no mind is intelligible either to itself or to another without such interpretants. These, however, are only fully known, as everything is fully known, in and through the community, which means that as isolated mind, or set of signs, man is a "mere" individual possessing no truth or reality.[49] Nor, says Peirce, can a given individual refute this by appealing to power or will as his essence, because identity is found not in the deed as such but in *consistency*, and this always involves something intellectual in character. Yet it is precisely on this account that the community is necessary, for, if the essence of man is to be a sign and signs require mediation for their complete interpretation, self-knowledge is ultimately meaningless apart from the community.

In the last of the papers mentioned, "Grounds of Validity of

---

pp. 516-519. For our purposes one section must suffice. "This final opinion, then, [referring to what the community of investigators discovers], is independent not indeed of thought in general, but of all that is arbitrary and individual in thought; is quite independent of how you, or I, or any number of men think. Everything, therefore, which will be thought to exist in the final opinion is real and nothing else. . . ."

[48] *Ibid.*, V, 353.

[49] Royce is more pluralistic than this, for he does not reduce man to his thoughts (Cf. *The Problem of Christianity*, II, Lect. X), although at times he is inclined to regard the attainment of truth as escape from isolated individuality, and salvation as salvation from "mere" individuality.

the Laws of Logic,"[50] Peirce again took up the community theme, this time in reference to the laws governing induction and deduction. What is of interest here for a study of Royce is Peirce's view concerning the relation between the individual and the community relative both to the process of attaining truth through logical procedures and to justifying these procedures themselves. Peirce disposed of the argument that the principle of syllogism is presupposed in any attempted deduction of it in a way typical of pragmatism. Just, he said, as a man may reason well without understanding the principles of reasoning, or play billiards well without a knowledge of analytical mechanics, so a man may perceive the force of an argument without knowing the general law according to which arguments hold good.[51] Regarding this as sufficient for his purpose, Peirce went on to define the general law of the syllogism as an explanation of the *suppositio communis*,[52] that is, no one who understands the meaning of the words denies that if A denotes all denoted by B, and B all denoted by C, then A denotes all denoted by C (when A, B, C are signs). Since the justification depends on what is commonly understood by the terms, the syllogism is warranted ultimately by the logical or scientific community.

The part played by the community in providing a warrant for logical procedure is even more marked in Peirce's discussion of induction. He stated the problem of induction as that of justifying the inference from part to whole. How, he asked, can we know from an examination of a part of a class what is true of the whole of it. For reasons which it is not necessary to set forth or examine here, Peirce rejected the appeal to what has been termed the uniformity of nature, and arrived at the conclusion

[50] *Ibid.*, V, 319f.

[51] This is true, but not strictly what is in question. It is often the case that questions as to what it is that is assumed in a given analysis are treated by pragmatism in a way which shifts the ground of the question. The question is: what is *presupposed* logically, not, what *can be accomplished* by assuming or without assuming certain things? See an excellent criticism of this frequent confusion in Russell's *The Philosophy of Leibniz*, p. 40.

[52] *Suppositio*—the *vox* as having this or that *significatio*.

that the generality[53] of synthetic or inductive reasoning rests on the idea of the "long run." If, according to Peirce, I take a handful of beans from a bag containing black and white beans and examine them to discover the relative proportions of each type of bean, any assertion about these proportions holding good for the whole bag depends upon the assumption "that, in the long run, any one bean would be taken out as often as any other."[54] Induction never possesses true universality, but only the analogue of universality and is alone warranted by the knowledge that in the long run reality (defined through the agreement of the community) will be discovered by this procedure, that is, our generalizations will continue to be verified. Concerning the truth of any single induction we cannot be sure, but concerning the community to which the "long run" of every induction is known, we can be sure that it provides a secure warrant for the inductive procedure itself. This is analogous to insurance practice, said Peirce; concerning a particular risk no certainty is possible, but concerning the security of the company in the long run one can be sure.[55]

Before abandoning this last paper there is one further idea in it, a corollary of the justification of induction, that is worthy of note. Peirce offered an ingenious argument to show that for the single individual no complete truth is possible on certain matters apart from self-identification with the community. "Each of us is an insurance company,"[56] said Peirce, for we must depend on our method of reasoning holding good in the long run, and if, as individuals, we possess a personal interest outweighing all others in some matter (analogous to the greatest possible risk assumed by the insurance company), then we are devoid of security on the theory of inference just developed and no valid

---

[53] That is, that they hold good in the future. See *op. cit.*, Sections 348, 349, 351.

[54] *Ibid.*, V, 349.

[55] At this point Peirce pointed out another aspect of the inductive problem which parallels Royce's discussion in the last lecture of *The Problem of Christianity*. This will be discussed in the appropriate place. Peirce's reference to the insurance company plays a part in Royce's idea of the insurance community. See Ch. VI.

[56] *Ibid.*, V, 354.

inference is possible for us. This means that to save the ground
of logicality the individual must sacrifice, in the interests of the
scientific community of which he is himself a member, whatever
personal interest he may have that would tend to destroy the
community which alone is the guarantor of truth and reality.
"So," Peirce concluded, "the social principle is rooted intrinsi-
cally in logic."[57]

Peirce rejected the subjectivism of individualism and sought
to point out that the community plays a much greater role in
the foundation of our use of reason than is generally recognized.
He who loses his private interest in self-sacrifice to the community
saves his own logicality and contributes to the advancement of
the completion of knowledge. Only the man who identifies his
interests with those of the community will attain truth. "That
ideal perfection of knowledge," said Peirce, "by which we have
seen that reality is constituted,[58] must thus belong to a community in which this identification is complete."[59] The individual, according to this theory, must either cast in his lot with
the scientific community or lose any chance of attaining a warrant
for his assertion.

The hope of the perfect community itself stands as justified
by one further consideration. Where our hope that we shall
survive, or that the perfect community will be realized and that
"What is Best will come about," is concerned, we are dealing
with the one interest in the universe which has no alternative
and for which no *reasons* can be given. In reasoning about this
no "long run" is conceivable because, said Peirce, *all* is at stake
and the matter is one of life or death in its seriousness. The hope
of success is the only rational foundation for action; it is thus a
logical necessity. This hope is infinite, to use Hegelian language,
in the sense that it cannot be identified with any finite or secondary hope, and has no "other," that is, there is nothing from
which it can be distinguished. "If its object were any determinate
fact, any private interest," concluded Peirce, "it might conflict

[57] *Loc. cit.*

[58] See *Collected Papers*, V, 311, for the statements of the meaning of "real."

[59] *Ibid.*, V, 356.

with the results of knowledge and so with itself; but when its object is of a nature as wide as the community can turn out to be, it is always a hypothesis uncontradicted by facts and justified by its indispensableness for making any action rational."[60] That such ideas form the true basis of Royce's theory of the community will be obvious when this discussion is completed.

It will be necessary to return to the ideas of Peirce later on in the inquiry. For the present the preceding brief statement of those ideas most important for the understanding of Royce's metaphysic must suffice. The Peircean background of Royce's later thought is not generally known,[61] despite Royce's explicit acknowledgement both of his debt to Peirce and of the general importance of the latter's ideas. Royce's view of the real world and his interpretation of Christianity in relation to that world represent the result of the application of certain discoveries made by both Peirce and De Morgan in the field of the logic of relations, to a concrete subject matter. This development is of particular significance at present for it is often taken for granted that the relational and purely formal view taken by modern mathematical logic is either opposed to metaphysics of any kind, or incapable of being extended to the analysis of specific subject matters. Royce's entire analysis in *The Problem of Christianity* shows the falsity of these assumptions and also illustrates the clarity and understanding which are possible when certain methods of refined analysis are employed in the investigation of particular aspects of experience which have often been but dimly understood.

Yet despite this the fact that Royce was dissatisfied, in at least one very important particular, with the purely formal representation of the infinite as defined by mathematics, should not be overlooked. In the essay appended by Royce to *The World and the Individual*[62] there is to be found an extended analysis of the problem of the actual infinite (particularly as posed by Brad-

[60] *Ibid.*, V, 537.
[61] Or, if known, it is certainly not taken seriously.
[62] *Op. cit.*, I, 473-588.

ley's discussion in *Appearance and Reality*)[63] based largely on
considerations drawn from the investigations of Cantor, Dedekind,
Bolzano, Peirce and others into the foundations of mathematics
and the theory of infinite collections. Royce argued there for the
actuality of the infinite as an orderly system definite in conception,
making use of Dedekind's deduction of the proposition, "There
exist (*es gibt*) infinite systems" in his essay, *Was sind und was
sollen die Zahlen*. It is unnecessary here to state and consider the
mathematical and philosophical problems involved. What is of
importance is that, despite all the ingenuity with which Royce
disposed of the criticisms of Bradley, Hegel, Bosanquet and others
regarding the unending or essentially defective character of an
actual infinite, and for all of his defense of mathematics against
critics regarding it as "abstract," he was still dissatisfied with
any purely formal representation of the infinite that does not
adequately grasp individuality. At this stage Royce accepted the
view that the infinite is actual as a well-ordered, self-representative
system. This indicates some development from his earlier view
of the Absolute as all-embracing unity of thought and harmony
of conflicting wills. What he still found lacking in the purely
mathematical conception of the infinite is a proper recognition
of purpose and the satisfaction of the will.[64] The Absolute must
be more than thought; it must be experience (immediacy) and
will at the same time if it is to be validly regarded as a self. With
this before his mind, Royce sought to solve the problem by conceiving the principle of order defining an infinite system as a
purpose. Royce saw that the attempt to conceive the infinite as a
determinate (and hence individual) totality must always be
defeated if such totality is made to depend on the system or series
in question having a last term. In order to avoid this difficulty
Royce adopted Dedekind's idea of the *Kette*, or infinite system,
as determined all at once by its definition, that is, the specific

[63] See, for example, F. H. Bradley, *Appearance and Reality*, p. 257, also *passim*
on the whole discussion of relations. See also B. Bosanquet, *Logic*, I, 177.

[64] In so far as Royce took will to be the true principle of individuation it can
be said that for him the Dedekind infinite still lacks true individuality. See *The
World and the Individual*, I, 581ff., and *The Conception of God*, pp. 250ff, 331.

order determining both the series as a particular whole and also each individual member. Royce did justice to his own voluntarism by interpreting the definition of an infinite series as the expression of a *purpose*. He said:

> The sense in which the series is a totality is, however, if the series is real, not at all the sense in which it merely has no last member. The series is not to be exhausted in the sense in which it is indeed inexhaustible. But you may and must take it otherwise. The sense in which it is a totality expressly depends upon that concept of *totum simul*, which I have everywhere in this discussion emphasized. . . . The *one purpose* of the perfect internal self-representation of any system of elements in the fashion, and according to the type of self-representation here in question, defines for any *Kette* formed upon the basis of that purpose, *all* of the ideal objects that are to belong to the *Kette*. And this purpose defines them *all at once*. . . .[65]

Thus, for Royce, the infinite is judged to be actual as a determinate totality in virtue of the fact that the definition determining a certain infinite system to be just this one and no other is the very same as the *purpose* or decisive will of that system. All arguments against the actuality of the infinite which are based upon the Aristotelian dictum that an infinite series cannot be "run through," that is, that it possesses no term which is "last," were taken to be false by Royce, because the reality of such systems as totalities does not depend on their completion in this sense. The definition of the series, that is, the formula or proposition defining its *order*, determines *all at once* all its members. By interpreting this definition as a *conscious purpose* or expression of will, Royce hoped to introduce the concrete content necessary to the conception of the Absolute as a Self who views himself as determinate. The Absolute for Royce is actual as a self-conscious Self, "not when it performs its last act, but when it views its whole wealth of life as the determinate satisfaction of its Will."[66] The true Self is infinite in detail and is therefore *many*; the true Self is determinate in purpose and is therefore *one*. For Royce, at this stage in the development of his thought, the one and the

[65] *Ibid.*, I, 582.
[66] *Ibid.*, I, 587.

many are therefore reconciled in the Absolute, because that Absolute Self knows the many as the precise expression of its own singular will and hence as determined in a unique way as an infinite totality.

The view of the Absolute as infinite system briefly sketched above represents a period in Royce's thought which lies somewhere between his earliest view of the Absolute as all-embracing thought that is appreciative in character and synoptic in its vision, and his most mature doctrine of the Absolute as a community of interpretation. It is clear that, by the time of the Gifford Lecture, Royce had attained the viewpoint of the Absolute as infinite system. The very fact that in those lectures he sought to supplement his view with the idea of will or purpose, so as to render defensible the belief in the Absolute as a self, suggests his dissatisfaction with purely intellectual interpretations of the Absolute.[67] A more concrete Absolute and one more adequate to both ethical and religious experience he did not attain until he came to envisage the infinite as a community possessing the definite triadic form of interpretation.

Thus far mention has been made of Royce's view of the Absolute particularly in its bearing upon metaphysical and epistemological issues. There remains, still by way of introduction to the central theme, the task of giving some indication of early studies made by Royce along decidedly practical lines. As is perhaps well known, he was greatly interested in the ethical and religious implications of what he called the spirit of loyalty and which spirit he summed up in the one fundamental principle of the good life, Be loyal to Loyalty. Since he regarded the particular analysis offered in *The Problem of Christianity* as an extension to the religion of Christendom of the more general considerations contained in

[67] See *ibid.*, Preface: "In my first book The Conception of the Absolute was defined in such wise as led me then to prefer, quite deliberately, the use of the term Thought as the best name for the final unity of the Absolute. While this term was there so defined as to make Thought inclusive of Will and of Experience, these latter terms were not emphasized prominently enough, and the aspects of the Absolute Life which they denote have since become more central in my own interests" (p. ix).

his studies of loyalty, especially *The Philosophy of Loyalty*,[68] it is necessary to set forth as briefly as possible the main outlines of the loyalty theme as it appears in the book just mentioned and also in several articles which were written at about the same time.[69]

Royce was always interested in an exact description of the relations among religion, ethics and philosophy. In accord with the voluntarism of his position he assigned an important place to the practical side of religion, or ethics, and yet, unlike the voluntaristic tradition, he did not neglect metaphysics but constantly demanded a rigorous theoretical foundation for religion. Concerning religion, he wrote in the preface to *The Philosophy of Loyalty*, "religion . . . has much to gain from the right union of ethics with a philosophical theory of the real world."[70] It would be correct to say that Royce's fully developed community theory, regarded as a theory of the nature of the real world, is an attempt to provide just such a metaphysical foundation for that spirit of loyalty which he considered to be the essence of religion.

Loyalty is defined very specifically as "the willing and practical and thoroughgoing devotion of a person to a cause."[71] This definition can be further clarified by a careful consideration of several terms in it, namely, "cause," "willing," and "practical." Loyalty must be devotion to some *cause*; it must be devotion which is *willingly* expressed (that is, the cause must be one of the individual's own choosing) and the devotion must be exhibited in some *practical* way. All of these elements are important to Royce's position, for loyalty "is never mere emotion" which it would be if it were a vague attachment to a dream or a wish, but true loyalty involves, besides affection, the metaphysical insight which justifies the end and the detailed empirical knowledge which indicates the means.

A cause (whether it is good or bad need not concern us at

---

[68] *The Problem of Christianity*, I, Preface.

[69] "What is Vital in Christianity " (1909), and "Loyalty and Insight" (1910), both from *Wm. James and Other Essays* (1912); also the Bross Lecture, *The Sources of Religious Insight* (1912).

[70] *The Philosophy of Loyalty*, p. ix.

[71] *Ibid.*, pp. 16f.

present) takes one beyond his own private experience precisely because it includes other individuals within its scope. For the loyal, according to Royce, the cause possesses an *objective* character in that, while it includes many individuals, it does not depend for its reality on any one of them, nor does its goodness consist in the fact that through its success the loyal individuals are fulfilled. "You, as one of the loyal, believe, on the contrary," said Royce, "that you love it (the cause) just because of its own value, which it has by itself even if you die."[72] In characteristic fashion Royce found the objectivity of the cause in its social character. A cause binds the many individual selves who are loyal to it together into a unity, but the cause itself has a super-individual character since it is never identical with any single individual. That this is the case, he contended, can be seen by reflecting upon the fact that the loyal are loyal not to others who are loyal (although this may be a concomitant state of affairs) but to the cause to which all are loyal together and which surpasses the individual selves on this account. If this were to be stated in Hegelian language a cause would be defined as that which is neither abstractly universal ("a mere idea") nor concretely particular ("a mere individual") but rather a concrete universal, or an actual but superindividual reality.

Passing on to the second element in true loyalty, the definite and free *willing* of the cause by the individual, the problem of the relation between the individual rational will and the wills of others is encountered. When the self is sufficiently mature to be aware of its own deeds, according to Royce, it recognizes that a truly good line of conduct can only be one which is consciously chosen and supported by the individual rational will itself. He said:

No external authority can give one any reason why an act is truly right or wrong. Only a calm and reasonable view of what it is that I myself really will,—only this can decide such a question.[73]

[72] *Ibid.*, p. 19.
[73] *Ibid.*, p. 25.

This marks the adoption by Royce of the Kantian principle of the autonomy of the moral will.[74]

Yet, as has been pointed out often enough in criticism of Kant, the abstract or formal principle of autonomy is not sufficient for the determination of any concrete course of action, since the question remains as to *what* line of conduct expresses this for a given individual in a given situation. Royce dealt with this problem, formulating it as one of self-knowledge or of understanding what the individual will contains of desires, inclinations, etc. However, he thought that neither an inner intuition nor the obedience to momentary caprice can enable one to find out his own will. No reflection on the variety of impulses constituting a self will reveal which one or ones should be basic, and no mere activity can suffice to indicate the principle upon the basis of which the whole range of desires is to be regulated. This leads, according to Royce, to a paradoxical situation: I must be the author and chooser of my life plan, the guiding principle of my life, and yet as an isolated individual I am never in a position to know my own rational will. He stated the difficulty thus:

> I and only I . . . can morally justify to myself my own plan of life. No outer authority can ever give me the true reason for my duty. Yet I, left to myself, can never find a plan of life. I have no inborn ideal naturally present within myself. By nature I simply go on crying out in a sort of chaotic self-will, according as the momentary play of desire determines.[75]

For Royce this difficulty could only be overcome when the social character of all life plans is recognized, and it was just here that Royce introduced a principle which plays an important role in his interpretation of Christianity: the principle that we come to know ourselves primarily through contacts with other selves and hence in discursive or mediate, rather than in intuitive, fashion.[76] He stressed the importance of imitation and its function

[74] *Ibid.*, p. 27.

[75] *Ibid.*, p. 31.

[76] One wonders whether Royce was acquainted at this time with Peirce's article on this theme. (*Collected Papers*, V, 213ff.) Dewey believes that the influence

in giving us our initial conception of who we are and what we are to do. Social training, he said, does not provide a complete solution however, for it is not only possible but highly probable that many plans will be discovered in this process, and we shall still be faced with the necessity of choosing among them. Only, at this stage, the problem of choice will have become more difficult because, according to Royce, in the course of social training our own self-consciousness will have been awakened and having our own way will appear more and more attractive. Royce apprehended a truth of which St. Paul spoke in his letters to the early church and which formed a basic part of his thought on human perverseness; the more highly civilized and integrated the community is, the higher the degree of self-awareness on the part of the individual members and the greater the possibility of self-assertion and rebellion against the same social structure which made that self-awareness possible.[77] Royce stated his understanding of this development as follows:

> Social training tends . . . to heighten by contrast our vague natural sense of the importance of having our own way. Social training stimulates the will of the individual self, and also teaches this self customs and devices for self-expression.[78]

Granting that social training leads to self-awareness and to the discovery of the rational will without which no *willing* choice is possible, the conflict between the individual and the corporate body remains. It is with this conception of the problem that Royce proposed loyalty as the supreme good and one which is able to bring about the reconciliation between the conflicting interests.[79]

---

of Peirce goes back to *The Religious Aspect of Philosophy* (*Papers in Honor of Josiah Royce*, p. 22 n. 2). Yet Royce spoke in the preface to *The Problem of Christianity* as if the ideas he discovered in Peirce came at a much later time and effected a change in his own thought. His remarks in *War and Insurance*, pp. 85-6, make this even more certain.

[77] This will be discussed further below. See *The Problem of Christianity*, I, 121, 144-150.

[78] *The Philosophy of Loyalty*, p. 34. Cf. *The Problem of Christianity*, I, 109-159.

[79] Students of Hegel and Bradley will recognize the similarity of Royce's

An exposition of the illustration offered by Royce at this point to indicate the function of loyalty will be found instructive.[80] Royce asked us to consider the case of one whose social conformity has enabled him to become adept at the art of speech and at influencing the plans of other men. Such an individual becomes proud of his power and is aware of his own self-reliance. He will be no natural enemy of the social structure which contributed to his success, yet he will be fond of being individual master and of having his demands recognized. A natural conflict consequently arises between the social and individual wills and no resolution seems possible on the basis of either one. At this juncture we are to suppose that there enters into this person's life some powerful emotion involving social ties such as patriotism, love and desire to serve and protect one's country, if need be, at the cost of life itself. The appearance of the demand for loyalty is what makes possible a breaking of the vicious circular struggle between the two wills. The following statement indicates Royce's view of the relation between the two sides: "The self looks indeed *outwards* for its plan of life. 'The country needs me,' it says. It looks, meanwhile, *inwards* for the inspiring justification of this plan."[81]

In the moment of self-devotion, he said, we find the two wills in harmony; the social will is served through the sacrifice of the individual (whatever concrete form this may take) and the individual is fulfilled because, to use the biblical expression, "He who loses his life shall find it." To obey and to serve the cause of our own choosing is to be true to the autonomy of the moral will at the same time that the opposition of the social will is overcome, for a cause is, by definition, a social enterprise.

The third element in loyalty, the *practical* expression of devotion, was of considerable importance for Royce, contrary perhaps to the popular view of what idealism implies. The good life is not one of purely spiritual devotion, according to the philosophy

---

statement of the problem and his proposed solution to the former's *Philosophie des Rechts* and the latter's *Ethical Studies.*

[80] See *The Philosophy of Loyalty*, pp. 38f.

[81] *Ibid.*, pp. 40f.

of loyalty, but it is always a life demanding some concrete expression dependent on the particular circumstances of time and place. Exactly what is to be done and how it is to be done is not a matter of *a priori* decision, but demands a direct acquaintance with the situation and as full a scientific knowledge of means to be employed as is available at the given time.

Loyalty must not be identified with martial virtues,[82] for it is capable of expression in many forms, religious, professional, commercial; indeed, it is present wherever there exists devotion to some cause which involves the cooperation and sacrifice of many selves. Loyalty is the core of the good life because it is the perfect illustration of finding one's life by losing it for the sake of that which is more than an individual. Self-realization demands unity and this in turn demands loyalty. It is on the basis of such considerations as these that Royce held loyalty to be not only good but the good.

Having indicated at some length the nature and function of loyalty as Royce conceived of it, the following three things yet remain to be dealt with before it is possible to turn to the theory that the community is the form of the actual infinite: (1) some statement of his argument for loyalty as the ultimate good, is necessary; (2) Royce's discussion of the meaning of truth and reality in relation to loyalty must be set forth; and (3) his view of the relation of loyalty to religion must be made clear. Upon the completion of these discussions, the background of the theory of community will have been sketched and it will be possible to proceed to a more systematic study of the nature and foundation of Royce's final view that the infinite is actual in the form of a community.

1. Royce developed the formula "loyalty to loyalty" as an expression of his belief that loyalty itself is the only good, for, first, only those who are loyal to some cause know truly the meaning of human life and particularly of their own life, and, secondly, the only cause that can be derived directly from the

[82] It is perhaps unfortunate that Royce chose the illustration he did since there are many others possible on his theory, and he offered them on other occasions.

recognition of loyalty as the good is the cause of extending or preserving loyalty. Yet just as Kant's ethic is beset by the difficulty that no specific good will in a specific case can be deduced from the rational will as good in itself, similarly, Royce's theory leaves us without an answer to the question: What particular cause shall I serve, granting that I want to serve loyalty? Royce recognized this and frankly admitted that the good life is not manifested in devotion to any cause indiscriminately,[83] and that no individual person can decide in his own case merely from the recognition of loyalty as the good. Something of a concrete nature can be arrived at, however, upon the basis of Royce's formula. At least the two general criteria that the cause chosen must not be destructive of loyalty and that it must provide the unity of a single life for all those attached by devotion to it, can be specified. For if loyalty is the good, then it must be extended and preserved; and if the good life involves bridging a gap between individual fulfilment and social claims, then the object of loyalty chosen must be such as is capable of bringing many selves together in the unity of a single life.[84]

Having set the problem of self-realization in terms of a self divided between purely individual wishes or desires on the one hand, and social obligations and goals on the other, Royce was led to find the solution in some good which leads to a harmony between the self and the world of which it is a part. Were the world already in fact a gigantic community of selves the fundamental opposition would be overcome. He recognized that this is obviously not the case, and hence Royce bade men to begin to serve the supreme cause by being loyal to some form of loyalty

[83] It is interesting to note that Royce evidenced a proper respect for the ambiguity of loyalty by his recognition of the possibility of its manifestation in evil and inhuman causes, and also its appearance in forms which lead to its own destruction.

[84] It has often been pointed out as a criticism of "community" theories of ethics that they involve social conservatism and preservation of the *status quo*. Such a charge has often been made against Hegel, for example, and against Bradley's famous "My Station and Its Duties" in *Ethical Studies*. Royce cannot be declared guilty on this account because he strictly maintained that unless the cause is *chosen* by the *individual* there is no real fulfilment. No acceptance of convention then is adequate, in his view.

necessarily involving the linking together of many selves. The uniting cause may be in the sphere of commerce or religion or politics or science, but the important thing is the community[85] to which loyalty leads and it is to that (some cause) that our devotion must be directed. One must bear in mind the number of different ways in which loyalty manifests itself. One may, for example, speak truly to another, and thereby exhibit loyalty to the cause of truth, which unifies the speaker and the one to whom he speaks. In this case the cause is truth and one expresses loyalty by speaking truly to the specific person spoken to. At the same time one is being loyal to a form of loyalty, which is the cause of those devoted to truth, and it is the community of such minds that ultimately guarantees whatever truthful communication human beings are able to achieve. As an illustration from the commercial sphere Royce chose the case in which fidelity has been exhibited by a corporation in some specific business transaction. Although it is obvious that such fidelity can never be exhibited except to particular individuals or groups at a certain time, yet any demonstration of honesty shows loyalty to a cause (ultimately as wide as mankind can be) which underlies all special transactions, the cause of honesty and confidence itself. In other words, loyalty to loyalty can and must be expressed through lesser loyalties in the concrete if loyalty itself is to prevail.

In both of the above cases loyalty to some form of loyalty is in evidence and this, according to Royce, is what finally succeeds in overcoming the opposition between the individual will and the social cause; for loyalty to loyalty in some concrete form serves to bring about the universal community embracing all mankind.

2. Just as the second volume of *The Problem of Christianity* is given over to a study of the relation between certain Christian ideas and the metaphysic Royce has developed, so a large part

[85] At this time Royce had not yet stated the nature of the community and the process of interpretation in precise logical form. Here the community was conceived in practical terms and not yet as a concrete embodiment possessing a certain logical form.

of *The Philosophy of Loyalty* is given over to a discussion of the metaphysical foundation of the ethic of loyalty and its relation to the nature of truth.[86] The same dissatisfaction with a purely moral idealism voiced in *The Religious Aspect of Philosophy* reappears. The good must be actual in some sense, according to Royce; its reality must not consist solely in some future state of affairs brought about by the earnest striving of the loyal. In this respect Dewey is correct in his judgment concerning Royce's absolutism, although it is made in the context of the problem of *choosing* ends. In his paper "Voluntarism in the Roycean Philosophy,"[87] Dewey characterizes the development of Royce's thought as a transition from voluntarism[88] to an intellectual absolutism, which latter position, according to Dewey, it was necessary for him to adopt in order to find "a rational measure of choice" for a will which is otherwise without direction. Since Royce refused to find such a measure in the *consequences* of certain intentions (which is why Royce is excluded from the circles of pragmatism, says Dewey) he must look for it "in some *pre-existing* Reality,"[89] which it is precisely the function of Royce's metaphysical analysis to find and justify.

Royce began the search for metaphysical foundations by noting a certain difficulty which his position as previously outlined had to overcome. "Loyalty to loyalty," he said, "doesn't seem ultimate. Is it not loyalty to all *objects* of true loyalty that is our ultimate duty? The object, not the relation, the universe and the devotion to it, not the devotion alone, is the object of our ultimate devotion."[90] In these words Royce stated what he regarded not only as a fundamental objection to his own position when considered as an ethic and nothing else, but as the cardinal difficulty of any "mere moralism" in which the attempt is made to

[86] What follows is discussed in Lect. VII, "Loyalty, Truth and Reality," of *The Philosophy of Loyalty*.

[87] *Papers in Honor of Josiah Royce*, pp. 17-26.

[88] Dewey has his own reasons which he believes are in accord with Peirce's thought for calling Royce a voluntarist and not a pragmatist. See *Papers in Honor of Josiah Royce*, p. 26.

[89] *Ibid.*, p. 26.

[90] *The Philosophy of Loyalty*, p. 303.

ignore ultimate questions of metaphysics by remaining on purely moral or practical grounds. The following section from *The Philosophy of Loyalty* states the problem fully but succinctly:

> A similar difficulty can be urged versus any mere moralism, that is, against any purely ethical theory of the moral life. One wants a doctrine of the real world, or a religion, to help out one's ethics. For . . . morality, viewed by itself, has a character that can well be suggested by the parable of the talents. The moral life, regarded simply as the moral life, is the service of a master who seems, to those who serve him, to have gone away into a far country. His servants have faith in him, but the service of his cause always has, for the moral, a certain mystery about it. They can indeed become sure, apart from any solution of this mystery, that their own supreme personal good lies in serving their lord. For not otherwise can they find even the relative peace that lies in a service of duty. But those who serve are not thus altogether secured against a pessimism regarding the whole outcome of human endeavor. For if loyalty is indeed our best, may not even this best itself be a failure?[91]

Royce's task was to show that loyalty is neither an illusion nor an instance of the pathetic fallacy, and he began by putting the question, "What must be true about the universe if even loyalty itself is a genuine good, and not a merely inevitable human illusion?"[92] Royce replied that if the possibility of spiritual unities of the type demanded by the nature of a cause can be justified, then loyalty would be shown to possess a basis in truth.[93]

The loyal individual, according to Royce, finds his personal good both by believing in the cause to which he gives himself and by believing that the cause itself is good (that is, that it is good beyond its function as that which provides his own particular realization). The question arises, in what sense can the good be said to be objective when located in the cause itself, since the cause is neither a particular nor a collection of particulars? In order for us to affirm the reality of the loyal man's belief,

---

[91] *Ibid.*, p. 305.

[92] *Loc. cit.*

[93] As will be shown, the same enterprise was carried on by Royce in *The Problem of Christianity* (Vol. II), which is consistent since he regarded Christianity as a special form of loyalty.

Royce answered, we must suppose actual "unities of spiritual life in the universe such that no man ever, by himself, experiences these unities as facts of his own consciousness."[94] If loyalty is well founded, Royce concluded, the causes which the loyal serve, the superindividual unities of selves, must be good in such a way as is never completely apparent to any of the individuals involved (nor to any collection of them). The reality of loyalty then requires the reality of a grade of consciousness surpassing in completeness and comprehensiveness that finite consciousness possessed by man. For such a consciousness the good experienced only fragmentarily by any single mind is complete. This argument for the consciousness for which what is good only fragmentarily for us is already complete is analogous to Royce's argument for the absolute thinker who possesses the truth as a whole.

It is well to take notice at this point of the method followed by Royce. He offered no "deduction" of loyalty as the good such as might be expected by a critic sceptical of the position. Aside from the demonstrable truth that no assertion indicating an ultimate good is *directly* justified by proof, just as Euclidean geometry offers no *direct* justification for its assumptions, it should be noticed that Royce merely sought to develop the metaphysical assumptions made by a believer in loyalty as the good, in order to provide an extra-ethical justification by showing the possibility of holding these assumptions to be valid. If the assumptions made by the loyal concerning the nature of the world and man's place in it are able to be defended on metaphysical grounds, then, according to Royce, the one who believes in loyalty as the ideal will have other than practical or ethical grounds upon which to maintain his view. As was noted earlier, and as Royce himself was aware,[95] the method followed is essentially the Platonic one of developing presuppositions in order to decide their status and their justification on the basis of considerations

---

[94] *The Philosophy of Loyalty*, p. 309. Cf. "Loyalty and Insight" in *Wm. James and Other Essays*, p. 55. See also "The Religion of Loyalty" in *The Sources of Religious Insight*, pp. 166ff. The unities in question here are the various communities of interpretation to be outlined below.

[95] See *ibid.*, pp. 306f.

relevant to such an inquiry. The "deduction" of the good on this view consists in showing the actuality of what is assumed, concerning the nature of the world and man's place in it, by those who believe in the good in question.

Having arrived at the superindividual mind constituting the basis of loyalty, Royce attempted to show the unity of loyalty and truth by establishing the necessity, as a condition of attaining truth, of the very superindividual unity under discussion. In this way, Royce believed, being loyal and seeking truth can be shown to be the same process viewed from two different vantage points. Since the loyal individual is caught up in that unity of selves which constitutes a grade of consciousness higher than that possessed by finite individuals, and similarly the truth seeker is a participant in a spiritual unity involving all those devoted to the cause of truth, Royce concluded that both good and truth imply the unity characteristic of a cause and cannot be regarded as wholly distinct. The possibility of showing the unity of loyalty and truth is ultimately connected with the possibility of showing the basic unity of the two elements in Royce which he referred to as the *absolute* and the *pragmatic*.[96] Despite his opposition to the pragmatist's definition of truth in terms of "workings" (consequences) and "credit values," Royce vigorously maintained the importance of the will as being at the foundation of all human enterprises, including the cognitive. "I assert," he said in the paper delivered at the International Congress of Philosophy in 1908, "all logic is the logic of the will. There is no pure intellect."[97] On the other hand, he hastened to point out, will does not dictate truth, that is, truth itself is not constituted by our decisions, for the simple reason that truth is not something factitious. Rather it is the result of a search for the structure exhibited by all things, and a search only to be carried on according to certain logical principles which are neither arbitrary nor dependent on human caprice. This is the absolutistic side

[96] Mention has already been made of Dewey's objection to allowing Royce to be called a pragmatist. But see *Wm. James and Other Essays*, pp. 208, 213, 253-54.

[97] "The Problem of Truth in the Light of Recent Discussion," in *Wm. James and Other Essays*, p. 234.

of Royce. By interpreting the search for truth as a moral activity, an expression of will, and by pointing out the inadequacy of ethics when not founded on truth, Royce hoped to show the complementary character of the good and the true. By calling attention to the superindividual unity implied by both loyalty and truth, he hoped to show an essential harmony between the striving to live the good life and the search to find the truth about the world in which we live.

Since the concept of truth plays such an important role in the philosophy of loyalty and is also of considerable moment in the articulation of the theory of community, some further exposition of Royce's view of truth, particularly in relation to that of pragmatism, will prove to be of value. In several of his writings,[98] Royce outlined his interpretation of the pragmatist theory of truth, referring mainly to James, and at the same time he also indicated what he regarded as the inadequacies of that theory. The following assertions may be taken as a summary of his understanding of James's position:

1. True ideas copy reality to a degree, but their power to do this is so limited that no adequate theory of truth can be content with the view that true ideas simply copy the facts or that they represent fixed relations between ideas and facts. The inadequacies of a copy theory prevent it from being the final word on the subject.

2. Verification is to be sought by reference to consequences, and this involves a comparison between certain ideas and certain other ideas, appropriate operations and states of affairs to which the initial conceptions direct attention. Royce quoted at some length from James to make this point clear.

True ideas lead us, namely, through the acts and other ideas which they investigate, into or up to or towards other parts of experience with which we feel all the while that the original ideas remain in agreement. The convictions and transitions come to us, from point

[98] "The Problem of Truth in the Light of Recent Discussion," *The Philosophy of Loyalty, The Problem of Christianity.*

to point, as being progressive, harmonious, satisfactory. This function of agreeable leading is what we mean by an idea's verification.[99]

3. Verification has a social aspect because no single individual verifies directly all that he accepts as true. This means that during the greater proportion of the time a given individual is founding his belief on *credit* values, that is, on the belief that certain truths are *verifiable*. The cash behind such credit consists in the fact that someone has, under stipulated conditions, actually carried out the verification. On this view, according to Royce, the truth of an idea is located precisely in its success in yielding the *cash*, whether a given individual accepts the verification performed by another or the justification of certain practical expediencies in his own experience which are not in conflict with other sensible experience or assured knowledge.

Royce then went on to indicate the heads on which he found himself in agreement with James' position as just stated. First, he agreed that the assertion of a truth is a deed, "a practical attitude, an active acknowledgment of some fact,"[100] and, secondly, Royce agreed that successful truth seeking consists in the finding of a practical congruity between assertions and empirical results. Hence if pragmatism means what Royce took it to mean, he must be acknowledged to be at least sympathetic with the pragmatic position. However, the other and absolutistic side of Royce, the side which caused James so much difficulty (and, of course, Dewey too) led him to raise certain questions concerning the adequacy of the pragmatist concept of truth as verification. It is worth noticing that the *concept* of *truth* is what is referred to, not the stipulation of a set of rules in accord with which certain propositions within the domain of a single science can be verified. When the question as to the nature of truth is raised, it is by no means evident that the answer is to be given in the form of an assertion stating *how we come by* warranted assertions. This is a crucial point in the critical discussion of both pragmatism and positivism, and one often overlooked. To discuss it fully

[99] *The Philosophy of Loyalty*, p. 319. No reference is given to James.
[100] *Ibid.*, p. 324.

would require a separate treatment; suffice it to say that Royce, like so many other philosophers before and since his time, was interested in the question of the nature of truth, such that even of any proposed method for testing propositions the question as to what view of truth is implied by said method might still be posed. Positivists generally either regard the latter question as meaningless or they point to the obvious *success* in certain domains of whatever theory of verification they mention, as ample justification of their view, hoping to evade the necessity of having to offer a definition of *truth* as distinct from verification in non-operational terms, or indeed in any terms. Royce was not asking what empirical procedure should be adopted for the purpose of verifying a given assertion or even all assertions of a given type (which information incidentally can be adequately supplied by the scientists in whose domain the proposition occurs without any help from philosophers even when these philosophers are "empiricists"), but what actually is meant by the term "truth"? In other words, Royce sought to provide a philosophical theory of the nature of truth. Nor can a theory of truth simply be regarded as unnecessary, for even if some method of testing the truth of propositions is advanced as the answer to the question, What is truth? the further question can still be asked, what assumptions as to the nature of both truth and reality are implicit[101] in that method? The meaningfulness of such a question for philosophers is not to be obscured simply because any particular answer which may be offered proves to be of no use for the purposes of empirical science.[102]

[101] By "implicit" is meant all propositions discoverable by analysis to be implied by the propositions stating the method although these propositions are not necessarily asserted in the statement of the method.

[102] The use of the basic idea of "Ockham's razor," or the principle of parsimony, to dismiss a great deal of the traditional domain of philosophy is one of the most ludicrous fallacies of our time. If certain philosophical theories and concepts are to be dismissed as "unnecessary," then it should at least be specified not only what "unnecessary" means in this context, but also it should be indicated "for what" and "to whom." To specify these means to raise the philosophic problems in another form since one is going to have to say "for scientific investigation" or "for the simplest explanation" or "to those committed to the view that metaphysics is nonsense."

Since the question of the nature of truth is of considerable moment for philosophy at present, it bears some further consideration even at the risk of destroying the continuity of the main discussion. Actually an analysis of the nature of truth is eminently relevant to a discussion of Royce's philosophy because his own position is so largely dependent on the concept of absolute truth. The central issue between positivism in all its forms and those who defend an explicitly philosophical theory of truth is whether or no truth can be exhaustively defined by a statement of *how* propositions *come to be* warranted or verified. That is to say, can the question, What is truth? be answered piecemeal by the specification of a method of verification? It would seem that at present a great many philosophers would answer, Yes. Royce and Peirce would undoubtedly have answered, No, and there is much to be said in support of their reply.

At the outset the question of geneticism, that is, whether a thing can be exhaustively defined by an analysis of the process by which it comes to be, must be faced and the answer must be that it is always false to make assertions of the form "A is nothing but B" where B is as complete an account of the coming-to-be of A as you please. This means that it is always false, when the nature of truth is under discussion, to assert that truth (A) is identical with ("nothing but") the operations (B), physical or symbolic, which must be performed in order that true propositions may result. Truth may be what is discovered, but it is not itself identical with some *method* of discovery, which is precisely why the question, What is truth? can not be answered by stating some *method* of verification.

Propositions are true when and only when what they assert is realized in some region accessible to human experience. The reference beyond the proposition, which in the case of true propositions properly constitutes their truth, is often covertly introduced, especially by positivists, through the ingenious expression "what is or is not the case." When the latter expression is employed, the "case," whether it is explicitly acknowledged or not, is *something*, Royce sometimes called it "wider insight with reference to which your own opinion gets its truth or its falsity,"[103] or "an infinite unity of conscious thought to which is present all possible truth,"[104] *which makes it possible that any specific proposition can possess the characteristic of being true or false.*

Further, Bradley is correct in his view that this is not changed at all merely by introducing the concept of the possible (the verifiable) or by appealing to what is actually the same thing, the "future." It may be the case that truth is *discovered* in such a way that we may always speak of a progression or a process from the present to the future, but again this is not the same as to affirm that the truth is *only* future where such assertion is meant to define truth exhaustively and to exclude the view that truth always is.[105] Royce would have agreed that the attainment of truth is always dependent upon the community of investigators and what they will discover to be the case in the "long run," and thus he accepted the appeal to the future, but he also maintained that the conditions making possible the discovery of truth in the future are not themselves only possible or future. These conditions are actual in that of them it is true to affirm that they always *are*, and in this respect they must be regarded as absolute or timeless. Many passages from Royce's thought might be given as illustrations but the following are particularly instructive:

. . . wherever two or three are gathered together in any serious moral or scientific enterprise, they believe in a truth which is far more than the mere working of any man's ephemeral assertions.[106]

This one Self, this unity of experience, to which we always appeal, cannot consistently be viewed by us as merely our own individual or private self, or as merely human; and its insight cannot be rationally interpreted merely as an insight into what is apparent, that is into what is not really real. Nor can it be viewed merely as something virtual—

[103] *The Sources of Religious Insight*, p. 110.

[104] *The Religious Aspect of Philosophy*, p. 424.

[105] See F. H. Bradley, *Essays on Truth and Reality*, pp. 341ff., for an excellent discussion of the point.

[106] *Wm. James and Other Essays*, p. 251.

a possible unity of experience, to which we would appeal if we could. In my opinion it must be conceived as *more* live and real and concrete and conscious and genuine than are any of our passing moments of fleeting human experience. It must be viewed as an actual and inclusive and divinely rational knowledge of all facts in their unity. And the very nature of facts, their very being as facts, must be determined by their presence as objects in the experience of this world-embracing insight.[107]

The conditions making truth possible are, for Royce, timeless or absolute in the sense that it is never the case that these conditions *will be* or that they *were*, but that there never is a time when the assertion "the conditions making possible the discovery of truth are themselves actual" is false. Much more analysis is required here, but to attempt it would entail a digression ruinous to the specific subject under discussion.

Royce centered his own criticism upon the question of the meaning of "success," and attempted to show that certain assumptions of the type he called "absolute" are contained within the pragmatist theory of truth taken by itself. If we grant, he argued, that there exists no purely theoretical truth, that is, a truth such as would in no sense guide a practical activity,[108] and that ideas must, when followed, fulfill our deepest needs, then truth must be inseparable from success in such fulfilment. The crucial question is, what constitutes success?[109] And this means that the question of the meaning of life cannot be evaded since it is impossible to offer a definition of "success" in which some reference to the goal of human existence does not appear. What we seek, said Royce, is self-fulfilment; to achieve this would be to succeed, but the problem remains as to what this is and where it is to be found.

Royce found the answer in the implications of loyalty. The loyal succeed, he maintained, or if they do not then no one does. And the loyal can verify for themselves individually their own fascination for the cause, yet since the true good is located in

[107] *The Sources of Religious Insight*, p. 123.

[108] See *The Philosophy of Loyalty*, p. 326.

[109] That no one at present seems to ask such a question is no doubt due to the illusion that everyone knows the answer.

the cause, which is by definition neither an individual nor a collection, the good is never experienced completely by any one individual. It follows that no individual ever possesses the cash value of the good in question. "If the cause exists, the treasure exists," said Royce.[110] The loyal do not base their belief on the ability to find the cash value of their chosen good in the present, for loyalty is sustained by a belief in a super-human unity of life, good in itself, such that no individual or collection ever experiences it fully, although this must not be taken to mean that as such the cause of loyalty is real *only* in the future.

Royce contended that the love and pursuit of truth implies the belief and striving of the loyal. Individually the verification of certain ideas can be accomplished by performing appropriate acts and thereby achieving success. Royce asked, however, "Can you express our human definition of truth in terms of any collection of our human experiences of personal expediency?"[111] and for purposes of examining the question, proposed the following illustrations[112] which are stated below, followed by Royce's comments:

1. A witness takes the stand and declares that, being a pragmatist, he will be sworn in only on the basis of his own definition of truth. He says, and here Royce exhibited his most penetrating wit, "I promise to tell whatever is expedient and nothing but what is expedient, so help me future experience."[113]

2. Suppose a sum of money has been left with another person by a person now dead, as a secret deposit to be returned at some future time. No evidence of a type which could be used to confute the recipient's denial of the transaction exists. The problem is, not what is the duty of the recipient, but what is the precise meaning of his telling the *truth* about the deposit in question?

Considering the first illustration, Royce maintained that we all mean something when we speak of the truthful testimony of the witness, but what that something is, is certainly not expressed

[110] *Ibid.*, p. 330.
[111] *Ibid.*, p. 331.
[112] The similarity of the second to Kant's famous example will be obvious.
[113] *Ibid.*, p. 330.

in the statement offered above. Royce believed that neither the judge nor the jurors, nor anyone, except perhaps the witness himself, would regard such a statement as descriptive of what it is to speak the truth in such a situation. The second illustration is more involved, but it fixes the point at issue very clearly. On pragmatic grounds, Royce argued, the witness may mean any one or all of three things by speaking the truth about the deposit.

1. He may mean to adopt the "forward-looking" attitude described by James.
2. He may mean to predict consequences to himself or to the estate.
3. He may consider that the truth of his statement consists in his own belief in his statement, or in the fact that he finds it congruent with his present memory.

On none of these possibilities, Royce believed, will the truth be reached, because the truth about the deposit does not consist in the attitude of the witness, nor in what he feels about his statement, nor again in any anticipated consequences to his own well-being or to that of another (where he is the sole judge of that). In short, what is meant by the truth about the deposit cannot be expressed in terms of the pragmatist theory, according to Royce.

Royce offered one further illustration in this connection which has to do with a postulate at the basis of knowledge. The assertion, "*Human experience, taken as a totality of facts, exists,*"[114] he claimed, is at the foundation of all knowledge, and its falsity entails the illusory character of knowledge, that is, the unreality of what it is that knowledge is knowledge of. Yet according to him this assertion is not verifiable in the same sense in which any assertion about a particular entity within that totality is verifiable. Royce anticipated two possible replies by pragmatists,[115] namely:

[114] *Ibid.*, p. 334.
[115] The ingenious reply that the question of verification, *in this particular case*, is meaningless had not yet occurred to anyone in James' day.

1. The assertion in question is not *verified*, but is accepted on principle as *verifiable*.

2. It is sufficient to trade on credit in view of the actual success following upon the assumption that such a totality exists, that is, in the "long run" belief in the continuity of experience is justified.

To these Royce replied, first, by suggesting the difficulty of the view that such an assertion is verifiable, and, secondly, by questioning the precise meaning of the "long run." The first reply supposes that the "cash," the actual verification, would come in the form of an experience not different in kind from that required for the verification of a particular assertion in, for example, physics. Were this the case, said Royce, verification would be impossible in principle[116] "since the very idea of the real existence of the experience of many men excludes, by its definition, the direct presence of this experience of many men within the experience of any one of these men."[117] Royce continued: "A super-human being, an union of the empirical lives of many men in the complex of a single experience,"[118] would be required to accomplish such verification, and this is certainly not a reality which those whom Royce criticized would acknowledge.

He considered the second possible reply for the pragmatist, the appeal to the "long run," as ample justification for belief in the continuity of experience, but held that it is inadequate as stated. In the first place he distinguished between the assertions, "This opinion is true" and "I just now find this belief expedient, it feels to me congruous." The former stands in need of some warrant which implies a concept of truth; the latter is merely a piece of personal biography.[119] Royce assumed that pragmatism

[116] And "verifiable" would be equally difficult to define, if it is not actually without meaning in this context.

[117] *Ibid.*, p. 336.

[118] *Ibid.*, pp. 336f.

[119] "Merely" in this context means that a scrap of biography is not relevant to a discussion of the nature and meaning of truth.

intends to speak of the truth of an assertion about the continuity
of experience in the former sense, and he therefore raised the
question of the precise meaning of the "long run." What is this
and when is it experienced? Royce asked. Is judgment made on
the basis of this moment or of some other? Does this type of
experience decide the question, or does some other? These are
all questions that must be answered if valid appeal is to be made
to the "long run." Royce ingeniously turned this difficulty of
pragmatism into an argument in support of the actuality of a
super-human consciousness. To appeal to the "long run" where
this concerns a given individual, is essentially the same on his
view as to appeal to a consciousness possessing a complete view
of that individual's experience. "Whoever," said Royce, ". . . .gets
the conspectus of my whole life, to see what, in the long run is
indeed for me expedient,—whoever, I say gets that conspectus . . . is essentially super-human in his type of consciousness."[120]
Even on the pragmatist view of truth, Royce concluded, there is
no escape from the eternal, since the "long run" is simply another name for that normative concept of absolute truth maintained by the idealist tradition since the time of Plato. Perhaps
something further on this point will be helpful. For Royce, the
"long run" was simply another name for the whole, or for perfection the possession of which constitutes truth. The "long
run" was indeed always future for him as it is for pragmatism,
but he differed from pragmatism in holding that the fact of its
being in the future has nothing to do with its being truth but
only with the mode of its *discovery*. In other words, on Royce's
view, unless one were prepared to maintain that truth is *made*
(and not only discovered) in the future, one must admit that
truth always is; although relative to its discovery it is always
beyond the present, that is, in the future.

The truth seeker, like the loyal individual seeks "a city out
of sight,"[121] and in loyally following after truth he is devoted
to a cause which is super-human in character and which is able
to bring the whole body of scientific investigators into the unity

[120] *Ibid.*, p. 339. Cf. *The Sources of Religious Insight*, Ch. VII.
[121] *Ibid.*, pp. 340f.

of a single life.[122] At any given moment our body of knowledge is incomplete because it falls short of the whole, but our recognition of it as incomplete is possible only upon the assumption that there is a conspectus which possesses the truth in its completeness. The "whole of experience," he said, possesses the truth, but no single individual has direct access to such a whole; nevertheless the assumption of its actuality is a necessary condition making possible any truth whatever. Again it cannot be pointed out too often that Royce was not concerned with the practical problem of specifying rules according to which specific propositions can be verified. Such rules are of the utmost importance and admittedly are not supplied by the type of philosophic analysis Royce offered. Certainly the metaphysical assumptions underlying the search for truth are not themselves *methodological* principles. However Royce was not interested in what physical or symbolic operations must be performed in order to carry out a particular verification, but only in what is assumed concerning truth and reality in the adoption of any particular methodology. For pragmatism to answer that no metaphysical assumptions are made is certainly evasive, as is likewise the attempt to dispense with the philosophic problems involved by regarding the answers to them as "useless." The latter evasion can be easily shown to be circular, since pragmatists will always define "useless" in a way consistent with their own operational view,[123] which is precisely what is in question.

Royce was also careful to guard against one fairly common misinterpretation at this point. It is not true, he maintained, that the eternal exists as a prior temporal order that it is the function of life to copy, but that the eternal order is discovered *within* the temporal in the form of that which makes knowledge possible.[124] This thoroughly metaphysical search for the *ordo*

[122] A detailed analysis of the structure of the scientific community will be given below.

[123] That is, concepts and answers to certain questions are judged "useless" on such a view when no direct contribution is made by them to specific problems of verification in the special sciences.

[124] *Ibid.*, p. 344. Cf. *The Religious Aspect of Philosophy*, p. 482. This is not the only form in which the eternal appears, as will be shown. Royce followed both

essendi distinguishes the Roycean enterprise from all purely epistemological, psychological or methodological investigations.[125] He rigorously insisted on the distinction between the order and structure of the actual on the one hand and the temporal order of the knowing process on the other. As William P. Montague has pointed out so well, it is of the utmost importance that the *ordo essendi* and the *ordo cognoscendi* be distinguished. Royce carefully distinguished the two, finding the former implicit within the temporal process, and hence discoverable within that process.

If the objection be made, Royce continued, that the foregoing analysis is erroneous, then the criticism can be shown to be circular. The argument here obviously depends on the previous analysis of error. For the possibility of error makes necessary precisely the absolute totality which would be denied by the objector. Royce stated the principle more fully in his paper presented to the International Congress of Philosophy in 1908.[126] There he said: "The absoluteness of the truths of pure logic is shown through the fact that you can test these logical truths in this reflective way. They are truths such that to deny them is simply to reassert them under a new form."[127] He thought this to be adequately exemplified in the case of the critic who urges the erroneous character of the analysis outlined above.

He finished the discussion of loyalty and truth with a humorous summation of his criticism of pragmatism and with a re-emphasis upon the similarity between the pursuit of truth and the pursuit of the good. The metaphysic of loyalty shows it to be allied with a unity essentially super-human in character as well as a unity that is actual and in which all our ideas are ultimately fulfilled. In this respect the search for and attainment of

---

Aristotle and Hegel in that he found the eternal implicit within the temporal. On this head the general truth of Hutchison Stirling's interpretation of Hegel in *The Secret of Hegel* may be noted.

[125] See *The Philosophy of Loyalty*, pp. 383f., for a full discussion of these differences.

[126] *Wm. James and Other Essays*, pp. 187ff.

[127] *Ibid.*, p. 244. The illustration offered by Royce is the Euclidean theorem that there is no last prime number. See pp. 247f. for the interesting voluntaristic turn which Royce gave to his view in distinction from that of Russell.

truth fulfills a need no less than any other pursuit successfully concluded. With a welcome touch of humor, Royce judged pragmatism in the following assertions:

A. It is bankrupt with respect to a foundation for truth.

B. It is afraid to go into the hands of a "receiver" because of the fear of absolutism.

C. It proposes to ignore these theoretical difficulties and to continue in business on the old style credit.

As was pointed out earlier, Royce regarded Christianity as a special form of loyalty, hence it is necessary to set forth his earlier view of the relation between religion and loyalty in order to present a complete account of his thought leading up to *The Problem of Christianity*.

The reality transcending human experience, which according to Royce we cannot but accept because our whole existence depends on the reality of other minds, accurate reports about past facts, etc., is neither dependent upon human experience, nor yet independent, if this latter means "independent of our experience." What transcends our experience must stand in some relation to it,[128] for the "real world is known to us in terms of *our* experience is defined for us by *our* ideas, and is the object of *our* practical endeavors."[129] On this view the real world is that region of live experience which fulfills the demand made by a proposition, thereby constituting its truth. The real world is not independent but "is of the nature of experience, whose structure meets, validates, and gives warrant to our actual deeds, and whose whole nature is such that it can be interpreted in terms of ideas, propositions and conscious meanings, while in turn it gives to our fragmentary ideas, and to our conscious life whatever connected meaning they possess."[130]

[128] It seems necessary to distinguish here between the "what" and the "that," essence and existence. *That* transcendent reality exists Royce admits, *What* that is can only be known in relation to our experience.

[129] *The Philosophy of Loyalty*, p. 362.

[130] *Ibid.*, p. 376.

According to Royce, the attempt to grasp this whole is expressed in the following way: the search for reality is the search to discover the whole of experience. Since the parts are known only in relation to the whole, success in the above enterprise contributes to individual self-knowledge, for each self is a part of the totality and its full meaning is contained therein. The task of each self is to find itself in the real world, the whole of experience, the content of the consciousness of super-human grade. From this it follows that the search for truth, the discovery of the details of the universal conscious life, is also an attempt to interpret the place of individuals within that all-embracing reality. Loyalty and truth are united, for the world acknowledged by both is one and the same. Loyalty to loyalty involves devotion to a unity than which there is no wider, for it embraces all men. Loyalty to truth is devotion to the same unity. The loyal are not deluded because causes "are real facts in the universe,"[131] and the real world (necessitated by the reality of truth) possesses the unity which universal loyalty seeks to express.

The object of religion, according to Royce, is the same united and self-possessed realm of reality perfected through the self-realization of the loyal. He interpreted the Eternal as identical with the conscious, super-human unity of life brought about by a cause, and consequently he regarded the traditional appeal to wonder-workers, psychic research and historical witnesses in support of the truth of religion as unnecessary. The object which religion seeks is found in the form of the unity to which the loyal are devoted and the truth of religion depends on the reality of such super-human unity. While loyalty seeks to interpret the Eternal in the form of deeds, religion is said to offer an "interpretation both of the eternal and of the spirit of loyalty through emotion, and through a fitting activity of the imagination."[132]

The interpretation of the Eternal offered by religion conflicts not so much with scientific knowledge, as Royce wisely pointed out, but rather with the demands of morality. The history of religion amply illustrates the conflict; in all the great religions

[131] *Ibid.,* p. 376.
[132] *Ibid.,* p. 377.

a central problem has been the correct interpretation of the moral aspect of the gods. The recorded experience of an Amos or Hosea, for example, or the criticism of the Homeric tradition to be found in Xenophanes or in Plato, proves this point.

For the purpose of making clear the relations between the two, Royce briefly outlined the two extreme views. It is often said that morality is remote from religion. This, according to Royce, may mean either one of two things:

1. When it is said in defense of *religion* the implication is that morality is "mere morality" and as such must remain on the level of merely human ideals, which level is insufficient precisely because religion seeks to pass beyond the merely human to the super-human.

2. When it is said in defense of *morality* the implication is that religion is superstitious and inhuman and a morality based on human ideals is sufficient. The assumption in both positions, according to Royce—and it is this assumption which is germane to this discussion—is that the human and super-human can be sundered, so that a cleavage between morality and religion must result. Royce rejected such a cleavage because he maintained both that the super-human is real and that it is capable of interpretation in human or reasonable terms. The interests of religion and morality can be harmonized, Royce believed, if a correct interpretation of righteousness can be achieved.

Royce suggested, paradoxically enough, that the situation of a "lost cause" makes possible the reconciliation of religion and morality. When the loyal come to the recognition that the cause to which they are devoted can never be perfectly realized in the finite experience of any one of them, then they must at once be aware that they are indeed seeking a city out of sight,[133] a reality which can be found nowhere but in the super-human. Royce extended this, maintaining further that sooner or later all causes are "lost causes," since no super-human unity can ever be brought to completion in a finite time, nor can it be fully expressed in transient human joy and successes. The fate of the loyal, then,

---

[133] *Ibid.*, p. 386.

is to lose their cause, for the world is incapable of expressing the ideal in its fullness. Royce ingeniously interpreted this as the metaphysical counterpart of the theological idea of the "lost individual." (See below.) The cause, he said, is lost to us because of the structure of human nature, or conversely human nature is lost and the cause is real in the higher world where the imperfection of human nature is overcome. Both assertions express the same religious truth.

The recognition by the loyal that their cause is lost produces a reaction of *grief* and *imagination*, responses which Royce characterized as the two parents of profound religion. Religious longing is expressed in these two forms, and through them the attempt is made to interpret the Eternal[134] in a way consistent with the demands of those whose loyalty is to loyalty itself, or, which is the same, the unity of all life. The symbolic and imaginative expressions found so abundantly in religious literature are intended to express the ultimate unity of life and in concrete terms. The rational analysis characteristic of the sciences provides the knowledge, and the only knowledge possible for us, of the details of the world and human life, but no such analysis apprehends the unity of life. It is this unity and how we stand in relation to it which imagination seeks to portray through symbol and metaphor. What Royce was particularly interested in pointing out is that the imaginative elements in religious literature may be and often are the result of special historical circumstances and motives, but that the absolute truth concerning the ultimate unity of life contained in religion abides despite the logical difficulties of the historical forms in which imagination seeks to express such truth.[135]

The foregoing account of those elements in Royce's earlier thought which are necessary for the understanding of his com-

[134] What this means will be more clear when the logical analysis of interpretation has been given in Chapter III.

[135] For example, as Royce noted in his discussion of Paul's thought, much of his theology is expressed in a form which experience has shown must be regarded as myth and symbol because dependent on the particular historical situation and the state of knowledge at that time. Yet he believed the *essential* part of Paul's statement of Christianity is defensible in metaphysical and ethical terms.

munity metaphysic contains implicitly the core of Royce's philosophy in all its aspects. The important point is that his dissatisfaction with a purely ethical or practical solution to the ultimate problems of philosophy, as stated in his first book, *The Religious Aspect of Philosophy*, leads to a demand for an actual or concrete infinite. The ideal or Absolute must not be left to depend on the strivings of those who believe in it, said Royce, but the Absolute must be shown to be actual. The search for the actual infinite ends with Royce's view of the community as the form in which such an infinite is real. On the basis of his studies pertaining to loyalty and religion, particularly Christianity, and also of the papers of Peirce briefly noted earlier, Royce came to the conclusion that the general triadic form of interpretation, and the various infinite communities made possible thereby, represents the actuality of the divine and hence the ground of all belief in the ultimate reality of God must be a belief in the reality of community.

CHAPTER THREE

COMMUNITY OF INTERPRETATION AS INFINITE SYSTEM

Before it is possible to understand what Royce meant by the "problem of Christianity" as well as by his central assertion that the community in its saving power is real, it is necessary to have a clear understanding of exactly what he understood by a community. This involves some analysis, logical, psychological and metaphysical, of such concepts as comparison, interpretation, time process and sign. In the examination which follows, the truth of William James' statement, to the effect that Royce made a greater effort towards clarifying and specifying the idealist tradition than idealists have generally done, should be apparent.[1] Royce's fully articulated theory of community stands as an excellent illustration of the results which may be achieved through the application of rigorous methods of formal logic to a concrete problem of the highest practical and theoretical importance.

Any attempt to analyze the relations between many selves, and thereby to indicate the nature of a community, raises the perennial philosophical problem of the one and the many, or, as it was most commonly stated at the time of Royce and James, the antithesis between monism and pluralism. Royce rejected this latter formulation when it entailed the view that there is a necessary disjunction between the two, for on his view a community appears as *both* one and many; the members are real as individuals and yet are linked together in a unity not identical with any one of them or with any numerical collection. In support of the reality of individual selves, Royce suggested three principles of individuation:

1. *The empirical sundering of feelings and immediate experiences*

[1] See James's remarks in *Some Problems of Philosophy*, pp. 137n, 138; also *A Pluralistic Universe*, p. 184.

cannot be denied. No individual, despite love and sympathy, ever feels the pain of another, although he may be aware of his own reactions to the outward manifestations (signs) of pain in another.

2. *The conscious intentions of one self can be discovered only indirectly by another self*, for one self can only possess the intentions of another if it becomes the other, which is clearly a contradiction.

3. *The active deeds of one self belong to that self and to no other in the same sense.* Each individual has his own destiny, his own rights, ideals and worth.

It would be a serious error, Royce said, to regard such individualism as "primitive," since it is the result of highly conscious cultivation and education. There is much anthropological evidence to support the thesis that in earlier periods of history the group or tribe is the primary entity, and in most situations it is the group that suffers and is guilty.[2] Individualism is thus a late tendency and reveals, among other things, the isolation of life from life.

Royce sought to pass beyond individualism, and hence he refused to accept these elements in our experience just indicated, as the whole truth. The problem of the community of individual selves, now that the reality of such selves has been shown, still remains. Royce wanted to know what we could say if we remain content with individualism, about the products of a community—language, customs, religions—in view of the fact that these cannot be regarded as the work of any identifiable individual. Languages and religions are not a collection of discrete phenomena, but they do exhibit certain unities upon the basis of which one may argue that they are characteristic of a single intelligence. The *unity* possessed by the social product, according to Royce, is what must be explained, and it cannot be explained by pointing

[2] It should be noted that Royce did not intend to raise the question of the primacy of the individual over the group or *vice versa* as a strictly anthropological or sociological issue. The history of the O.T. community or of the Greek City State is sufficient evidence in support of his contention here, and a more thorough study is not necessary.

to the activity of any individual or collection of individuals. It is necessary to conclude, then, that the community possesses a mind of its own, or at least that it possesses a characteristic which functions in this way.[3] For again, if the individual selves are separated from each other, and Royce has given good reason for maintaining that they are, how can the community behave as if it possessed one common intelligence?

At this point Royce turned to James' discussion, "The Compounding of Consciousness," in *A Pluralistic Universe*, in which the latter dealt with the problem of more inclusive states of mind or, more specifically, how one mind might be inclusive of another.[4] Roughly stated, James' view in that chapter is that, despite difficulties in the theory that there is any *actual* compounding of consciousness, some type of reality must be accorded to states of mind more inclusive than a single conscious state if we are to explain even certain obvious facts within the experience of one mind, although to admit such reality is irrational.[5] Royce interpreted James to be in fundamental agreement with Bergson in holding to the basic unity of all consciousness which only appears in the form of separate selves because of the abstracting power of the intellect.[6] James pushed his inquiry no further than this, but Royce was not satisfied and believed that the former had merely stated the problem in another way.

Royce took it as a basic characteristic of the community that it has a special relation to the temporal process. A community

[3] Royce made use of the material of Wundt and Bastian, the German psychologist and ethnologist, respectively, whose lectures he heard when in Germany. Further study of the relationship might be revealing for historical purposes, but Royce's philosophic theory must finally be judged in the light of certain other considerations.

[4] It is well to remember that James' discussion did not cope with all the problems being considered by Royce at this juncture.

[5] James frankly admitted that the experience of some wholes is not to be explained as a combined experience of parts. See *A Pluralistic Universe*, pp. 185ff.

[6] This is indeed a strange conclusion for James in that the individual selves are not ultimately real on such a view, nor could a "pluralistic universe" be real either.

speaks of its past when it refers to deeds and accomplishments that have remained within the memory of its present members.[7] A community also has a future because its members look forward to the achievements of certain common goals expressed as its common hope. A community, Royce concluded, is "essentially a product of a time-process" (*The Problem of Christianity*, II, 37), and this is the first specific characteristic definitive of what it is to be a community. A casual crowd, although it may have a mind and will, possesses no institutions, no history and no common customs. Its members have no common memory *as a group*, nor do they look forward to any common goals which are anticipated only in virtue of their being members of this group. A crowd is distinguished from a community because it has neither a common memory nor a common hope. A necessary condition for a community, then, is a remembered past and an anticipated future.

An excellent illustration of the relevance of history to the community can be found in the record of the Old and New Testament communities. Royce appealed to this record in answer to a possible objection, but he could not present as complete a case as might be presented on the basis of those assured results in biblical criticism which are now available. He rightly saw that Paul had interpreted the life of the Christian community to which he spoke as a part of the great spiritual drama of history beginning with Adam, passing through Moses and the prophets and culminating in the appearance of the Messiah. Thus the Christian community has a common memory, the mighty deeds of God and his promises in the past, and also a common hope, the actual fulfilment in the future of those promises in the perfect community of spirits, the kingdom of heaven. Contemporary biblical scholarship insists upon the continuity of the old and new Israels, or the Old Testament and the New Testament church,[8]

---

[7] This "past" or common life of a community is easily enough illustrated in some of our present attempts to write "international" history. The existence of what is little else than national history makes this a somewhat difficult task.

[8] It is well to bear in mind the etymology of the word "church." It is from ἐκκλησία "those called out," hence the community of those committed to God's word. See Robertson, *Regnum Dei*, p. 316.

and also that the Christian community is not intelligible except through explicit reference to the life and faith of Israel.[9]

The function of the common past and future in making community seems clear enough, but Royce offered an interesting analogy which makes the significance of the time process striking. His analogy is between the individual self and any form of corporate life. At any given moment each individual is confined to a mere fragment of the self, the fragment which can be found at *present*; since the self has existed in the past and will continue to do so in the future, the datum in the present can never be more than a fragment. The self of the present is linked to the past in memory, and is also aware that whatever the past is, it is the past of just that self. It is in this continuity, said Royce, that is to be found, in part, the identity of the self as well as that which actually guarantees the distinctness of the many selves. Such continuity of memory, however, is not the whole of the self, for that which links the present self in coherent and significant fashion to former experiences cannot be overlooked. Following one of the ideas of Peirce[10] that the self is never a simple datum, nor just a collection of data, Royce maintained, "my idea of myself is an interpretation of my past,—linked also with an interpretation of my hopes and intentions as to my future."[11] Both from the standpoint of a given self and of certain others who come in contact with that self, interpretation is a necessary condition of there being a self at all in any *significant* sense. In the former case, the individual interprets his past to his future self, and in the latter the other selves judge an individual's present activities in the light of his past deeds and experiences. In either case the self is the result of interpretation. Following Royce's analogy, if we attempt to estimate the relations between

[9] See, for example, N. H. Snaith, *The Distinctive Ideas of the Old Testament*, Preface and p. 204; W. F. Albright, *From the Stone Age to Christianity*, pp. 280, 302ff.

[10] *Collected Papers*, IV, 225ff.

[11] *The Problem of Christianity*, II, 42. It will be remembered that Mary Calkins, always an admirer of Royce's philosophy (See *Papers in Honor of Josiah Royce*, pp. 54-68), centered her objections on the Peircian idea that the self is not a datum but an interpretation (which means also an achievement).

a great many selves and the past, the idea of the community will inevitably enter; for the possibility of many different selves at a given time having identically the same past as is constitutive of their own past selves individually, is readily seen when a conscious effort at interpretation is made. In any random collection of persons many of them would discover, through a conscious process of interpreting their past, that a part of their selves coincided with a part of a great many others. From the strictly empirical standpoint, Royce said, the persons in their given existence would remain as real as any pluralist or individualist could wish; there would be no mystical merging of the selves or interpenetration of consciousness tending to obliterate the individuality of any self. Yet the fact remains that, when the process of interpretation has been completed and certain identities of past experience have been brought to light, the selves involved are linked together in such a way that they can say, "We are of the same community." On this view, community depends on the interpretation of certain facts, and, as Royce noted, there is nothing essentially mysterious about it, since it is exhibited every time some one considers part of some history in relation to his own personal history. The community is actual when the process of interpretation leads two or more selves to recognize that a common element is part of their own individual pasts. Upon such recognition, said Royce, "they may be said to constitute a community *with reference* to that particular past or future event."[12]

The foregoing analysis depends so obviously upon certain more formal considerations concerning the self formulated by Peirce in a paper[13] mentioned earlier, that it seems worth while to set forth and examine more carefully what it is that both Royce and Peirce were asserting. Peirce raised the question of an intuitive self-consciousness, asking specifically whether knowledge of "I," as distinguished from both consciousness generally and pure apperception, which is intuitive in character, is possible

[12] *Ibid.*, II, 50.

[13] "Questions Concerning Certain Faculties Claimed for Man," *Collected Papers*, V, 213ff.

for us. Prior to putting this question, Peirce asked a preliminary one, if by simple contemplation of a cognition, apart from both previous knowledge and signs, it is possible to judge whether a given cognition refers to its object immediately, or whether it has been determined by a previous cognition. He answered this question in the negative for the following reasons:

1. The necessary distinction between having an intuition and knowing intuitively that it is an intuition further necessitates that no part of a given cognition will be the answer to the question concerning whether or no it is an intuition.[14]

2. There is no doubt a *feeling* that individuals possess such a power, but the inquiry whether the *feeling* is itself intuitive presupposes an answer concerning the original question. This line of attack therefore leads to an infinite series and no resolution is reached.

3. Historic facts must be appealed to and this type of evidence shows that we do not possess the ability in question. Peirce offered the following support for his contention:

(a) Witnesses are often unable to distinguish between what has actually been seen and what is their own interpretation (or their inference).

(b) Before more accurate analysis it was thought that the third dimension of space was directly intuited; now it is known to be an inference.

(c) A man can distinguish textures of cloth, but he needs to move his finger over the surface, thereby involving comparison, which is mediation.

On the basis of these arguments Peirce decided that it is impossible to judge whether a given cognition refers to its object immediately, or whether it has been determined by a previous cognition, simply through contemplation without reference to previous knowledge or to signs. This negative answer makes it

[14] Peirce defined "intuition" as cognition determined by something out of consciousness, or "nearly the same as 'premiss not itself a conclusion' " (*Collected Papers*, V, 213).

impossible to decide whether self-consciousness is intuitive or not without appeal to evidence. Peirce believed that all knowledge of the self is mediated by the testimony of others. This testimony enables us to discover our ignorance and our errors, both of which necessitate our supposing a self in which these inhere. Peirce even went so far as to make ignorance and error the distinguishing characteristics of the concrete individual self: "Ignorance and error are all that distinguish our private selves from the absolute *ego* of pure apperception."[15] Peirce concluded that since there is no necessity to suppose an intuitive self-consciousness, it can be judged to be the result of inference.

Further, Peirce raised the question of a power of introspection and whether or no knowledge of the internal world is wholly derived from external facts.[16] By "introspection" he understood "a direct perception of the internal world but not necessarily a perception of it *as* internal."[17] In consequence of his rejection of an intuitive power of deciding the status of cognitions, his answer to the present question had to be decided by the circumstance that the relevant facts cannot be explained without assuming the reality of a power of introspection. Peirce believed that the following illustration settled the point: the exhibition of anger over something in an individual implies something in the object (according to his view of that object) as occasion for the response. Peirce's point is that the anger consists in the assertion, "This thing is vile," etc., and hence is a predicate of the not-self, since it is referred to the object. It is only upon reflection that the individual says, "I am angry." Hence emotions are either predicates of an object, the not-self, or they are determined by previous cognitions. In either case, according to Peirce, the facts can be explained without recourse to the power of introspection. Peirce raised a final question, which is perhaps the one most pertinent to this discussion: whether or no we can think at all without signs.[18] The most obvious answer is that we can, for, he said,

[15] *Collected Papers*, V, 235.

[16] *Ibid.*, V, 244ff.

[17] *Ibid.*, V, 244.

[18] *Ibid.*, V, 250ff.

thought must precede every sign, assuming of course, the impossibility of an infinite series. Ultimately he answered to the contrary, however, and for the following reasons: Intuition will not decide the question; therefore the appeal must be to external fact. Thought can only appear as an external fact in the form of a *sign*, hence all thought must be in signs. From Peirce's definition of a sign it follows that thought involves mediation in the form of many minds or of a process of discussion in one mind. In the article on "Sign" in *Baldwin*, Peirce defined a sign as "anything which determines something else (its *interpretant*) to refer to an object to which itself refers (its *object*) in the same way, the interpretant becoming in turn a sign, and so on *ad infinitum*."[19] A thought, therefore, addresses itself to another, that is, to one which interprets the sign which that thought is, and this involves a *process*. There is no thought in an instant, which is precisely why an intuition involves no thought, for all thought is in signs, and all signs must be interpreted.[20] A process of mediation is necessarily involved. As he put it, "To say, therefore, that thought cannot happen in an instant, but requires a time, is but another way of saying that every thought must be interpreted in another, or that all thought is in signs."[21]

There can be little doubt of the correctness of Peirce's reasoning in the above analysis, although obviously it all follows from the definition of "intuition" and of "sign." The former is by definition not a sign, and the latter is by definition such that it could never be an intuition. The power of distinguishing between cognitions, or of introspection, or of intuitive self-consciousness, can never be intuitive, because on this view signs are always involved in making such distinctions and these require mediation. Recognition of this does not destroy the correctness of the analysis however, since the definitions offered by Peirce are not arbitrary but may be regarded as real definitions. It must be admitted that self-knowledge involves mediation in some

[19] *Baldwin's Dictionary of Philosophy and Psychology*, II, 527, col. 2.

[20] "Interpretation" has been used a great many times up to this point, without definition. A detailed analysis of its structure is offered below.

[21] *Collected Papers*, V, 253.

form, since immediate apprehension (intuition or introspection) will never yield *knowledge*, for even if signs are the result of such apprehension, an interpretation will be required and immediacy must be left behind. Royce agreed with Peirce's analysis that the self is no datum which is given at an instant as an intuition, although he did not agree that ignorance and error alone constitute individuality.

One difficulty with this fundamental position as adopted by both thinkers was noted by Peirce in passing.[22] This difficulty is seen by defenders of the view that knowledge of the self is the result of intuition. Royce held that discursive knowledge of past deeds and intentions is necessary in order that there be any concrete self at all. That such interpretation or mediation is necessary if the content of the self is to be known, cannot be denied, for all that constitutes a concrete self is certainly not given by any immediate, non-discursive apprehension of that self by itself. However, it is difficult to see by what process of mediation one could decide whether a given element (event, deed, intuition) is or is not a part of the past of a given self, unless the existence of a self aware of signs were already presupposed. That there is a self at all cannot be derived; either it is apprehended intuitively or it is not, for there is no premise from which it is possible to infer that a self exists unless it be presupposed at the outset. On the other hand the necessity of discursive thought for knowledge of the *concrete content* of the self cannot be denied; the arguments offered by Peirce and Royce seem conclusive; still, a given self aware of signs and capable of interpreting must be presumed to exist before any reference to the past or possible future of such a self can be made at all. W. E. Hocking has made a similar criticism of Royce's theory of the self: "As every interpretation, including a theoretical first one, presumes the existence of the minds addressed by the interpreter, the belief in the existence of minds beyond my present self cannot be a *product* of interpretation."[23] He should have gone on to point out that the same

[22] *Ibid.*, V, 237. "Our own existence cannot have been inferred from any other fact."

[23] *Harvard Theological Review*, VII (1914), p. 111. See J. M. E. McTaggart, *Philosophical Studies*, Ch. III.

criticism may be urged not only in the case of other minds, but with respect to the interpreter's mind as well.

The above point can also be made with reference to signs. There is no sign which upon interpretation asserts the *existence* of something unless such existence be assumed at the outset. All the signs, the interpretation of which results in self-knowledge, touch upon the nature or concrete content of a given self. That a self exists, that it is its own self, can never be the result of the interpretation of any sign, but must be known immediately by the self in question or it is never known at all.

This digression has been necessary in order to indicate the logical foundation of Royce's view that the self depends on interpretation, and is, like the community, intimately bound up with the passage of time. At an instant there is no self, for Royce, but only a fragment, the fleeting content of the moment which is itself forever passing away. The reality of the self depends on an interpretation of its past, just as is the case with the community, and also, as will be evident in the course of the discussion, the self depends on the community since, if the interpretation of signs is a process of discursive thought, other minds must be involved.

Royce proposed, on the basis of the preceding considerations, to use the term "community" in the more restricted sense of a unity based on common elements of experience, both past and present. Many selves may be said to constitute a community when they have an ideal common past and an expected future. This may be represented schematically as follows:

$$E_f.$$
$$\text{Hope.}$$
$$\nearrow \qquad \nwarrow$$
$$S^1_{pr.} \quad \rightarrow \quad S^2_{pr.}$$
$$\searrow \qquad \swarrow$$
$$E_{pa.} \qquad \text{Memory.}$$

S_1 and S_2, selves in any portion of time which they may both regard as present, constitute a community of memory or of hope in virtue of the fact that they possess certain events, E_f or E_{pa}, as common parts of their individual selves. Memory, however, is fallible[24] and it is difficult, Royce admitted, to set limits to the self of the past. Consequently a warrant of some sort is necessary in order that a reason may be given for accepting or rejecting past deeds. The ideal extension of the self is not arbitrary, for limits must be set on rational grounds, and in the case of a given self such limits can be defined only by the self in question. The important point for Royce is that whatever limits are set depend on the interpretation one puts on oneself, and these interpretations ultimately define the community or communities to which that self belongs.

The conditions which Royce considered necessary for the occurrence of the community may be summarized thus:

1. The community must have a goal and it must attempt to reach this through appropriate deeds which belong both to all the members because part of their ideal selves, and to the community itself.

2. The community must be capable of communication within and among its members.[25]

3. In the ideally extended selves of the community some events must be present which appear identically throughout all.

Royce regarded the third condition as the one capable of the most exact description and he offered an analysis of the way in which the Christian community satisfies it, but this will be dealt with in Chapter V. It is sufficient at this point to indicate more fully the importance of the last-named condition.

[24] It will be remembered that Hume (*Treatise*, Bk. I, Pt. IV) rejected memory as that which constitutes the identity of the self because it cannot retain all that has occurred.

[25] Royce noted that he emphasized this condition lest he be accused of ignoring the distinctness of the members. There is, he said, no "reduction or melting of these various selves into a single merely present self" (*The Problem of Christianity*, II, 67). See *The Philosophy of Loyalty*, p. 395 for the same idea, but cf. both with the following statement characteristic of Royce's earlier and less pluralistic position: "The world of life is then what we desired it to be, an organic total; and the individual selves are drops in this ocean of the absolute truth" (*The Religious Aspect of Philosophy*, p. 441).

Cooperation involving many selves is not a sufficient mark of the community, according to Royce, unless such common endeavor involves the process of interpretation as well. The true community is one in which the members not only *love* it, together with its past and its anticipated future, but also they understand the part which they are to play in the successful completion of such goals as may be projected and striven for. To put this another way, community implies cooperation with interpretation, and if this second element is absent the result is the merely highly efficient organized corporation in which there are many individuals who "cooperate," but who, being virtually unaware of the meaning and purpose of the whole enterprise or of their particular significance in it, are little more than cogs replaceable by other cogs without any appreciable change in the entire structure. For Royce, the community ends when the gigantic web of interpretation breaks down, for then the spiritual link between the selves is destroyed and what remains is an unconscious mass of beings who work, but who, in the highest sense, know neither who they are nor what it is that they are doing.

Yet, Royce was perfectly aware of the fact that both the complexity of the community and the weakness of man in his tendency to place his own individual interest uppermost in his thoughts are factors which render any actual community far from perfect. This implies that some power is necessary which can preserve the community in its remembered past and hoped for future, since the level of ideal interpretation cannot be maintained. Because human interest falters, because strife enters the community for countless reasons, because the vastness of the community makes complete understanding on the part of each individual impossible, some force from beyond the situation is necessary if the community is to be preserved. Royce found this power in *love* for the community and all that is bound up with it. Love is loyalty and ultimately it passes beyond understanding because it is able to perform what may be and often is impossible on the level of understanding. Love turns the community into the Beloved Community,[26] which was, for Royce, the ultimate community.

[26] See *The Problem of Christianity*, I, 172.

Perhaps at this point the basic rationalism of Royce is most apparent, for he came close to interpreting love as itself a kind of insight, thereby making it a species of knowledge. The preservation and completion of the community which love effects would thus seem to be a completion of knowledge, that is, that in love we somehow understand or have insight which we did not possess before. It is true that he warned against using the term "love" to indicate a mystic insight or union,[27] and consequently he emphasized the practical aspect of love as love for the deeds of the community and as the striving to attain the successful completion of such deeds. Despite such emphasis, Royce still spoke of the fulfilment made possible by love as if it were a fulfilment of knowledge and even went so far as to suggest that the Pauline expression $\alpha\gamma\acute{\alpha}\pi\eta$[28] contains within itself the idea that in love can be seen a fuller or more adequate "meaning" than is possible without it. The significant point for the evaluation of this theory is that Royce would be most surely attacked for having made *partial insight* (a form of ignorance) the prime evil from which men need to be "saved." That a more complete insight than man ever attains in history is implied in the Christian view of salvation cannot be denied,[29] but that the love existing in the Beloved Community provides merely a fuller knowledge which is intended to save men from a state of ignorance or partial insight, is seriously open to question, historically as well as systematically. Royce is not as guilty of such rationalism as many who today interpret him as a "shallow" and "optimistic" idealist would maintain,[30] yet there is no doubt that his thought exhibits a tendency in that direction.[31]

[27] *Ibid.*, II, 96.

[28] Royce's analysis of $\alpha\gamma\acute{\alpha}\pi\eta$ is dubious in itself. He sees it as an "emotion" which longs to see complete what is only fragmentary at a given time, and also as a longing for some mystical union. Neither of these would correctly characterize $\alpha\gamma\acute{\alpha}\pi\eta$ as intended by Paul in his letters.

[29] See such passages as I Cor. 13: 9ff., esp. 12.

[30] See for example, *The Problem of Christianity*, II, 102, where he explicitly said that love for the community is not the same as knowledge of it. See *Hibbert Journal*, XII (1913), pp. 215-220.

[31] See particularly *The Sources of Religious Insight*, where, despite the recognition

Frequent use has been made thus far of the term "interpretation," particularly in the analysis of the self and of the community,
and it may be gathered from such usage that interpretation denotes
a cognitive process of some sort. Precisely what that process is
must now be explicated since the basis of the community, for
Royce, is to be found in the nature of interpretation. It will be
remembered that in Royce's time the philosophical issue of perception *vs.* conception occupied a place of importance which it
no longer holds. This is not to suggest, as many believe, that, on
the one hand, there is or was no real problem involved, or that
we at present have reached a satisfactory solution, on the other,
but it is important when discussing historical views not to lose
sight of the fact that what may appear as a problem at one time
also appeared at another, perhaps in a different guise, and in
philosophy this means formulated in a different way. The issues
between rationalists and empiricists may still be drawn, but the
perception/conception formulation of one of these issues does
not hold the central place it held when Royce and James carried
on what R. B. Perry has so aptly called "the battle of the Absolute."

Royce recognized the prevalence among philosophers of the
perception/conception dichotomy; he cited Bergson's position
as an instance of a dualism in which these alternatives are regarded
as exhaustive, with Bergson choosing a kind of perception as
the important and essential way of knowing. Royce was mainly
interested in calling attention to the assumption that the alternatives presented are in fact exhaustive. He suggested at least the
possibility of a third type of cognition which can be accurately
characterized neither as perception nor conception. A type of
cognition triadic in character, hinted at but never clearly developed
by Kant, furnishes the key to Royce's attempt to emerge from
the impasse. Kant developed a triadic pattern in his philosophy—
sense, understanding, reason, corresponding to perception, conception, reasoning—although, as Royce correctly said, it is only
in the *Kritik der Urteilskraft*[32] that Kant offered any consistent

---

that "insight" involves more than theoretical knowledge, the end of religious
"salvation" is taken to mean the possession of the most perfect insight.

[32] It is interesting to note that Hegel also regarded Kant's third *Critique* as

statement of the constructive character of "judgment." With this in the back of his mind and with the aid of certain logical principles formulated by Peirce, Royce set out to define with utmost precision this third type of cognition which he called *interpretation*.

Ideally, he said, we can define both a perfectly pure perceptual knowledge (although as Bergson's philosophy shows such definition would have to be *ostensive* in character) and a perfectly abstract conceptual knowledge (such as might be illustrated by a system of geometry dealing with figures possessing only one side and one edge). No matter how carefully we endeavor to remain, for the special purposes of science or philosophy, within the confines of one domain or the other, we are forced to recognize that actually the intelligent life of an individual person involves *some* synthesis of the two types. Simply to call attention to this fact is insufficient, for he thought that the exact type of union involved must be analyzed and clearly formulated. To resort to the idea of an active or practical union is inadequate for two reasons: (1) The logical form of such a synthesis is not specified, and (2) such a solution already makes the assumption that the disjunction, either perception or conception, is exhaustive. Royce therefore proposed to show first, the falsity of such a disjunction considered as exhaustive, and, secondly, the necessity of a third type of cognition which is not reducible to (a) perception, (b) conception, (c) some combination of a and b, (d) a synthesis of a and b in action. A third type which can fulfill these conditions is *interpretation*.

In order to establish the inadequacy of the distinction between perception and conception when considered as exhaustive, Royce proposed the question: Within which of the two domains would another mind and the active processes of that mind belong? The mind of A is, for B, neither a *datum* (however "hard") nor an *abstract character*, since no perception had by B, and no abstract character known by him is identical with the mind of A. Royce expressed this in the language of pragmatism:

the most important of his writings and the one closest to the truth. See *Logik* in *Encyclopädie*, Sec. 55.

1. B can produce no cash value for A's mind.[33]

2. B cannot identify A's mind with any universal abstract idea he knows.

Royce believed that there is a third type of cognition, interpretation, which is not definable in terms of perception or conception alone, and which is adequate to the task of defining a mind. In order to make the point more clear Royce offered the following illustration:

If a traveller arrives at a boundary provided with (A) Gold coins (perceptions) and (B) bank notes (conceptions), he may discover that while both A and B are good on one side (that is, on the side *from which* he travels) neither A nor B are good on the other (that is, the side *to which* he travels); A is not legal tender in the country q to which he goes, and although B is convertible into A, A is not legal tender in q. The difficulty can be overcome only if a process which is neither the presentation of A, nor the attempted conversion of B into A is introduced. The process C of *interpreting* A in terms of whatever it is that corresponds to A in q, is exactly the process required.[34]

All processes of communication are analogous to this process of interpretation which is a distinct type of cognition. Whenever one mind C takes up the task of interpreting A to B, a process is required which is analogous to that of the traveler going into the foreign country and faced with the necessity of interpreting his cash in terms of what corresponds to cash in the new country. The mind C must attempt to communicate to B what is essentially the mind of A. This process may be represented schematically:

A. Self   B. Self

C. Interpreter

C, the interpreter, receives signs which signalize A, and he pre-

[33] That is, unless we identify that mind with something we are prepared to call "cash value" from the outset. At any rate, A's mind is *not identical with* whatever it is that we decide furnishes us the cash value.

[34] *The Problem of Christianity*, II, 130f.

sents an interpretation to B in terms of whatever signs in B's experience would enable him to understand A. Hence C says to B, in effect: What I say to you is what A says, and A and B are thereby linked together by some common understanding through the efforts of C. The point which Royce was particularly anxious to make is that just as the process of obtaining cash for bank notes is different from the process of exchanging coins for foreign coins at the border, so is the process of verifying concepts by obtaining percepts[35] different from the process of interpreting other minds. Interpretation is a distinct cognitive process which possesses a structure all its own, and it is indispensable to the life of the individual since almost all specifically human relations require it. Three illustrations not given by Royce may be offered in order to clarify the actual function of interpretation.

1. A student of philosophy is faced with a difficult passage of Kant, let us say, and an instructor is called upon to assist the student in understanding the passage. The instructor encounters the text which is for him a set of signs including percepts, concepts, feelings, etc., and on the basis of this he offers an interpretation. He, in effect, says to the student, I believe that what Kant said is what I am now saying to you. That is, the instructor mediates the mind of Kant, accessible to him through signs, the text, to the mind of the student.

2. A candidate for some political office faces the necessity of stating his views on the nature of democracy and of democratic institutions. Anxious to prove himself a loyal and able supporter of the tradition in which he stands, he selects some classical exponent of his view and proceeds to interpret that writer to his audience, saying, in effect, what I say to you is what so and so says.

3. A theologian interested in showing the relevance of his religious faith to some contemporary problem of importance states certain ideas or principles of his religion and proceeds to set forth their meaning in relation to some problem at hand.

---

[35] No matter what specified operations must be carried out to achieve this in a given case.

In this way that religious tradition is interpreted and the preacher is saying in effect: in this particular case my religious tradition says what I have said.

In each of the above human situations the process of interpretation is illustrated and Royce is undoubtedly correct in holding that in no one of such cases have we simply the problem of verifying concepts by discovering the appropriate percepts. Perceptions, conceptions, feelings, etc. are no doubt made use of in the process, but the structure of interpretation is such that it cannot be fully reduced to these processes of cognition.

One element in Royce's illustration of the traveler going into the foreign country is of particular significance and that is the relation between the structure of interpretation and the dimensions of time. Interpretation, it is said, is directed to the future in the sense that an interpretation is what is called for when we find ourselves in situations where our ideas borrowed from the past no longer "work," or where it is not clear in what particular direction the successful "working" is to be found. When we face periods of transition, when we "cross the boundary," to use Royce's expression, an interpretation is called for, because it is of the greatest importance that we should understand if possible the new signs (experiences) that come to us, by reference to our present ideas. This temporal significance of interpretation needs to be more fully considered, but first the essentially *triadic* nature of interpretation must be elucidated, for the two are closely connected.

An interpretation necessarily requires three terms and does not consist simply in stating a dyadic relation between two terms. When, for example, it is asserted that "a is to the left of b," it is clear that the relation "to the left of" is a dyadic relation. Interpretation, however, is *triadic* in character because a mediator between two minds (signs) is required and this mediator must itself function like a mind (sign). The following illustration drawn from the domain of archaeology will make this clear:

If a tablet is found which is in a language different from that (or those) spoken by the discoverer, a translator is clearly required and his task is to set down the tablet in the form of a language different from the original one. Schematically this may be represented as follows:

A. Egyptian text   B. (Translation)
   (Signs in the form   Possible
   of an inscription)   English reader

                    ↖   ↗
                 C. Translator
                  (Egyptologist)

C interprets A by providing the equivalent of A in language understandable by B. The translator mediates through his translation between the original signs and the possible English reader.

The type of relation exhibited, according to Royce, is *non-symmetrical*, since C must know both A and B and any change in the structure in a specific case would result in the loss of interpretation.[36] Thus three terms are a necessary condition of interpretation.

The fact that interpretation is triadic in character is important to Royce's theory, because for him the three terms correspond to the dimensions of time, past, present and future. This temporal relation[37] is readily seen when it is borne in mind that interpretation always involves the consideration in some *present* of signs which are past and which are to be interpreted by other signs addressed to a *future* mind. This is clearly illustrated by Royce's own example in reference to self-knowledge: a man remembers a past promise by calling to mind what he meant to do at that time, and to his future self he addresses the command to perform

[36] This does not mean that the terms may not be exemplified by different minds. For example, A may be interpreter and B possible reader or vice-versa. This is of great metaphysical importance because, in Royce's view, God may be either interpretation (Logos), interpreter (Spirit), or signs to be interpreted (Being).

[37] The key to this relation is in Peirce's idea that there is no thought in an instant. See *Collected Papers*, V, 253.

that line of conduct which brings the original promise to successful completion. Schematically this might appear thus:

A. Past self—Promise   B. Future self—The
                                            self to whom the
                                            command is ad-
                                            dressed

                    C. Present self—
                       Interpreter

C, in commanding a certain line of conduct to B, says, in effect,
What I say to B is what A says (translated into the form of appropriate action), and the three terms of interpretation are correlated
with the three dimensions of time. It is noteworthy that, when
Royce proposed metaphysical generalization from the logical
structure of interpretation, he wisely left the "authority of
Peirce"[38] behind and claimed that he alone was responsible for
the metaphysical views advanced. Briefly stated, his view is that
all reality is essentially a process in which the *present* interprets
the *past* to the *future*. Past time, for example, is constituted by a
realm of events[39] the traces of which are present in historical
records. Interpretation of such records is carried on by present
historians and embodied in other records which are addressed
to the future. Or again, to use Royce's illustration, the geologist
studies some natural phenomenon, the Grand Canyon, let us say,
and in doing so he is confronted with certain natural phenomena
which are themselves records of what has taken place in the past.
The geologist who is able to read these signs, that is, who knows
what inferences can be drawn from the evidence, interprets them
for future geologists, who will in turn interpret these signs in
the light of further evidence.

On the basis of such considerations, Royce proposed to view

[38] *The Problem of Christianity*, II, 144.

[39] It is important to note the "realism" here, that is, the past is not the same
as its traces in the present, but is actually constituted by a "realm of events."
See *Ibid.*, II, 145.

the world as recording its own history, and time as itself an
order of possible interpretation. "The triadic structure of our
interpretations," he wrote, "is strictly analagous, both to the
psychological and to the metaphysical structure of the world of
time."[40] The fact that every interpretation is addressed to the
future and also that it is itself a sign necessitates that the process
of interpretation be *infinite* in character, that is, there is no proposed interpretation not a sign, and hence no interpretation fails
to stand under the condition of requiring a further interpretation.
Interpretation, according to Royce, always needs three terms and
the result is a sign which calls for the process to be repeated,
unless we possess an interpretation which is final, which would
be the same as absolute truth. Since no such finality is possible
in any domain, interpretation never ceases. Royce says, "and so,—
at least in ideal,—*the social process involved is endless.*"[41] This is
precisely the form in which the infinite is actual, namely, as the
universal community of interpretation which is without end.[42]
It is important to note in this connection that, for Royce, there
is no danger of time becoming unreal, since time correlates with
the structure of interpretation itself. Royce urged this against
Bergson's view that the dimensions of time are arbitrary and the
result of the "static" intellect.

Perception and conception are both self-limiting processes for
Royce and this is the very thing that marks them off from interpretation, for, while perception and conception are either lonely
or sterile, interpretation is a conversation and finally leads to
what neither one of these can produce alone, namely, a view of
God, the universe and man's place in it. Since a sign, as distinct
from an icon or an index, according to Peirce's formulation in
the *Baldwin* article, necessarily implies an interpreter, and since

[40] *Ibid.*, II, 147.

[41] *Ibid.*, II, 149. (Italics not in original.)

[42] *In re* the Hegelianism of Royce it should be noted that Hegel would surely
regard this position as an instance of the "bad" infinite. Many passages from
Hegel could be cited, but one in connection with the syllogism is instructive in
this context. See *The Science of Logic* (Trans. Johnston and Struthers), II, 310.
Cf. McTaggart, *Commentary on Hegel's Logic*, paragraph 220. See Royce's remarks
in *The World and the Individual*, I, 527n. 1.

all actual interpretations are themselves signs, the process of interpretation must continue without end, unless a particular chain of interpretation is interrupted by death or by separation of the individual from the community. "Therefore," said Royce, "it is not the continuance, but the interruption of the process of interpretation which appears to be arbitrary; and which seems to be due to sources and motives foreign to the act of interpretation."[43]

It may be that at this point, as Loewenberg has pointed out,[44] Royce's theory of community can most easily be shown to be a fulfilment of that determinate infinite the nature and conditions of which he set forth at such length in the "Supplementary Essay" to *The World and the Individual*. According to Loewenberg, the community of interpretation can validly be taken as an infinite system of the type Royce envisaged. He says:

> It is not mere endlessness, however, which constitutes the nature of interpretation. Its endlessness is one which any self-representative process exemplifies. It is the endlessness of a determinate infinite which Professor Royce has expounded in the "Supplementary Essay" to *The World and the Individual*.[45]

Loewenberg correctly notes that, while Royce did outline a metaphysic of interpretation in *The Problem of Christianity*, he did not refer explicitly to his earlier definition of infinite systems. Yet there can be little doubt that the community of interpretation fulfils the conditions of an actual infinite as Royce defined it, both in virtue of the fact that interpretation calls for a sequence of interpretations which has no last term (interpretation), and also because this infinite sequence is an expression of the *will* to interpret and the endless sequence is given all at once as the unending sequence which expresses that purpose. It is in this sense that the community of interpretation is a true infinite;

[43] *Ibid.*, II, 151.

[44] See his Introduction to Royce's *Fugitive Essays*, Cambridge, 1925, and *The Philosophical Review*, May, 1916, pp. 420-423, which contains a note on interpretation.

[45] *Philosophical Review*, May, 1916, p. 421.

the unending sequence of interpretations involved in all the social endeavors of mankind is, for Royce, an expression of the will to interpret, and as such this sequence is given in its entirety at the moment when the community is initiated.

Nevertheless Loewenberg rightly regards the series of interpretation as a self-representative one and the symbolic formulation which he offers in this respect is instructive, though it stands in need of correction in some significant particulars:[46]

(1) Let x = any sign
    Let y = any interpreter
    Let z = any interpretee (This term was not used by Royce, but is introduced by Loewenberg following the analogy of *addressee*.)

(2) Then R (x, y, z) = any interpretation, that is, the triadic relation which unites the sign, the interpreter, and the interpretee into a complex.

(3) But the triad, R (x, y, z) is in turn a sign, requiring interpretation.

(4) The new complex will be R $[R (x, y, z)]$ $y'z'$ . . . .

While this formulation seems to express Royce's view, there are imperfections in it, which should be removed. First, in Step (2), R (x, y, z) cannot properly be taken as the interpretation. The unity of the terms is the *form* of the cognitive process but it is not the cognition or interpretation itself. Loewenberg sees this and in a note[47] he calls attention to the fact that Royce used the term "interpretation" to denote both the *process* of cognition and the *result* of such a process. This is true, but it is clearly the interpretation as *result* that stands in need of further interpretation and not the triadic form or unity of the process. Thus Step (3) needs to be modified also since R (x, y, z) is not itself the sign in question here, for the simple reason that the triadic relation is not what is to be interpreted, but rather the interpretation

[46] What follows is from *Philosophical Review*, May, 1916, pp. 422-23, with some slight modifications.

[47] *Ibid.*, p. 422n. 4.

which such a relation yields. It is true, as Loewenberg adds, referring to interpretation, that "this result, though now a single 'sign,' is logically the compound of previous sign, interpreter, and interpretee,"[48] but it is nevertheless true that the interpretation as *result* is the sign standing in need of further interpretation, and that this can and must be considered in itself apart from the logical structure of the process from which it results. Furthermore this is the very sense in which the future community of interpretation will consider the result of previous interpretation, that is, without conscious reference to the fact that the sign to be interpreted was itself the result of a former triad.

With these considerations in mind the following formulation will be seen to be more accurate:

(1) Let x = any sign to be interpreted
   Let y = any interpreter
   Let z = any interpretee
   Let I = any sign which is a resultant interpretation
(2) Then R (x, y, z) → I = the triadic relation uniting sign, interpreter and interpretee into a complex yielding I as the interpretation of x.
(3) But I is in turn a sign, requiring interpretation through the triadic relation R (I, y' z') → I'
(4) The process continues without end, and the form of the series is determinate in that each term is a triadic relation whose *purpose* it is to interpret that interpretation which was the resultant of the previous triadic relation.

It was precisely because the element of purpose was so emphasized by Royce in the community of interpretation that he himself did not furnish us with the analysis of the community as self-representative system in the strict sense. It is more appropriate to characterize the endless chain of interpretations as one in which the one *purpose* of interpretation is expressed because each new triad of interpretation sets out to interpret the sign resulting from the previous triad. This means that the will to interpret (in any

48 *Ibid.*, p. 422.

particular case you please) stands as the basis of the chain which follows, and that such a will can only be completely expressed through that series of interpretations each triadic term of which interprets the sign left by the *preceding* triad, thereby bequeathing a new sign to a possible *succeeding* triad. To be true to Royce's voluntarism this endless process must be seen as a necessary part of the expression of the one will to interpret. Furthermore, it is not difficult to see that it is particularly the social character of interpretation (that is, that interpretation is the interpretation of "somebody to somebody") which gives the community of interpretation a concrete character for which the purely formal infinite of Dedekind can make no provision.[49]

Interpretation alone is what is adequate to the task of understanding spirit in the multiplicity of human situations which involve "the successful interpretation of somebody to somebody."[50] Both perception and conception fall short of the mark because the self is not so constituted as to be grasped by either of these functions. The fact that interpretation manifests the nature of its object fits it for the task of understanding spirit, for spirit, according to Royce, is fundamentally social in character and requires the interrelation of many minds. Spirit or life, precisely because it is social in character, can never be reduced, just as interpretation can never be reduced, to either perception, conception, or any theoretical or practical combination of the two.

There can be little question of the basic truth of Royce's contention that conscious life is infinitely richer than either seeing or conceiving. Mankind, in its intelligent and therefore most exalted existence, has as its primary concern neither the having of perceptions, nor the apprehending of abstract characters, but rather engages in the search for ever new and more fruitful interpretations of God, of the universe and man's place in it. In the light of this consideration Royce suggested a further criticism of Bergson's doctrine of intuition. He was aware that it is not the function

[49] It is of course understood that Dedekind's formal analysis stands under no obligation to provide for any such metaphysical considerations as Royce sought to introduce.

[50] *The Problem of Christianity*, II, 151.

of the artist, for example, to perceive in immediacy, but rather to *interpret* life, presenting his interpretation in sensory form. The prophet likewise, said Royce, must pass beyond seeing and abstracting, and literally discern the *signs* of the times, and perhaps, if he be inspired, even of all time. In this respect Royce's position has the great merit of calling attention to the vital function of interpretation in all conscious human endeavor, and of seeking to employ a most exact analysis of its logical structure to its actual operation in the most subtle and most significant human experiences.

Interpretation may be accurately styled as "living reason" (although Royce does not use this expression himself), for it grasps exactly the logical structure of a more or less conscious process employed constantly in the course of actual human experience, in the broadest sense of that term you please. The person who, in the midst of solving some practical problem seizes upon a solution after careful reflection, performs what is essentially a cognitive process of interpretation, and the result is always some truth which can be said to have evolved from other truths, experiences, etc. assumed as already had. It is the logical form of the discovery of new truth and fresh insight into the nature and meaning of existence that was Royce's central concern in the entire discussion of interpretation. He sought to analyze the structure of reason in its life, as it moves through the world endeavoring to discover that system of relations which constitutes whatever precise knowledge exists.

It is in the process of interpretation that reason shows forth both its capacity as living and its ability to function within the experience of beings for whom history is real, and who look to the future as well as to the past as they attempt to understand themselves and their world, and to achieve whatever fulfilment is possible for them in it. One should bear in mind this living function of reason, for it was to show the relevance of interpretation to problems of religion, ethics and metaphysics that Royce took pains to present so careful and extended an account of its logical structure; at the same time he was aware that the *actual* process in living experience is not completely conscious and so of course not analyzed. In his illustration of the two men rowing together in a boat, Royce referred to their *common* boat as an explicit interpretation, which nevertheless is only known as an interpretation through analysis. In referring to the idea of a *common object* generally, he said:

> This is an interpretation; but it is an early and a natural interpretation. So long as we are untrained to reflection, we remain indeed unaware of the principles which lie at the basis of such common-sense opinions about natural facts.[51]

Augustus De Morgan, in the paper mentioned previously,[52] criticized the narrowness of traditional logic in its restriction of relations to those of identity, non-contradiction and excluded middle, and he did so for a reason directly connected with the subject under discussion here. De Morgan did not reject the validity of the relations stated, but he regarded them as providing a basis so narrow as to make it impossible to *distinguish* or evolve one truth from another. In the course of the discussion, De Morgan suggested that in actual thinking, that is, in the making of distinctions and in the discovery of implications, certain combinations of relations must be employed which do not fall within the scope of the traditional class inclusion and exclusion relations.[53] From this paper it is quite clear that De Morgan was calling attention to the same idea of the "third" or interpretant, necessary both in making a distinction between notions and in discovering their implications, that Peirce spoke of in his paper,[54] and which was used so effectively by Royce for his own extralogical purposes. De Morgan had said, "Any way of speaking of one notion with respect to a second, joined with a way of speaking of the second notion with respect to a third, must

[51] *Ibid.*, II, 246.

[52] "On the Syllogism No. IV and on the Logic of Relations," *Cambridge Philosophical Transactions*, X, 331-358. See an interesting illustration of the significance of a relational view cited by Royce from De Morgan in *The Sources of Religious Insight* (p. 92).

[53] This is the same as saying that ordinary syllogism is only one instance of combination of relations.

[54] "On a New List of Categories," *Collected Papers*, I, 545ff. Peirce himself mentioned this paper of De Morgan's (*ibid.*, 562).

dictate a way of speaking of the first notion with respect to the third.''[55] In commenting on this statement Peirce remarked:

"These last [referring to predicates having three correlates] (though the purely formal, mathematical method of De Morgan does not, so far as I see, warrant this) never express mere brute fact, but always some relation of an intellectual nature, being either constituted by action of a mental kind or implying some general law."[56]

It is interesting that Peirce believed he had extended the analysis made by De Morgan beyond the scope of formal logic, and that Royce carefully pointed out his intention to amplify these ideas further by advancing a general metaphysical thesis based on them.

As a further preparation for his metaphysic of interpretation, Royce proposed to enlarge upon the psychology of interpretation,[57] and also to give some indication of the ideal which guides the truth-loving inquirer. The process of *comparison*, said Royce, following the analysis of Peirce,[58] is an elementary form of interpretation which, because it is relatively simple and free from the complications introduced by our social efforts to communicate with other minds, is useful for beginning the analysis of interpretation in its more complex forms. Comparison is not a *dyadic* relation, but a *triadic* one; on this both Royce and Peirce insisted. When a contrast or "otherness"[59] is encountered, the idea of the respect in which terms or states of affairs are compared must be employed, and this means that a "third" or interpretant is always introduced. Although Peirce offered several excellent illustrations, and Royce one unwieldy one, to make the point clear, De Morgan had given an example which is superior to both, and is worthy of

[55] *Cambridge Philosophical Transactions*, X, 347. See *The Sources of Religious Insight*, pp. 96f., where Royce calls attention to De Morgan's recognition of the importance of relation in logic.

[56] *Collected Papers*, I, 301-302.

[57] It is well to remember that since, for Royce, interpretation is of the essence of philosophy, a consideration of it remains at the same time close to his main theme.

[58] Royce referred here to the paper entitled "On a New List of Categories," *Collected Papers*, I, 545ff.

[59] *Ibid.*, I, 553.

consideration on that account. Speaking of comparison, De Morgan said:

> Any two objects of thought brought together by the mind, and thought together in one act of thought, are *in relation*. Should anyone deny this by producing two notions of which he defies me to state the relation, I tell him that he has stated it himself; he has made me think the notions in the relation of *alleged impossibility of relation;* and has made his own objection commit suicide. Two thoughts cannot be brought together in thought except by a thought: which last thought contains their relation.[60]

The truth of the general thesis that no comparison is possible without a "third" can easily be shown both in common speech and in more refined analysis. If one were to draw two plane figures, a circle, (A) and an ellipse, (B) on a sheet of paper and ask a person not versed in mathematics to compare them, it is highly probable that he would reply by saying that B looks like an egg, while A does not because it is "round." It is obvious that the comparison is attempted by introducing a rough notion of *shape* such that a statement is made about both A and B in relation to their respective shapes. A more refined comparison would involve the notion of the size of the major axis in relation to the minor, such that in the case of A the axes (*radii*) would be equal and in that of B the major axis would, as its name implies, be larger than the minor. Actually the idea of "shape" as a third or mediating idea making the comparison possible is employed in both cases, since the relative sizes of the axes is what determines the "shape" (or we may say that in this case it is a precise formulation of the vague expression "shape").

Whenever explicit comparisons are made, said Royce, we have two distinct ideas before us standing in need of being put in relation and which may be as varied as the following:

a. Different percepts or concepts.
b. Clashing interests or motives.
c. Contrast of art forms.

[60] *Cambridge Philosophical Transactions*, X, 339.

d. Two warring passions.

e. Contest between plaintiff and defendant.[61]

This list should serve to make clear the wide range of application Royce assigned to the terms "comparison" and "interpretation." In all these situations a cognitive process of the same logical structure is involved, but this is not to say that comparison or interpretation is confined to any one type of situation or to one which is strictly intellectual or theoretical in character. In concrete conflicts, estrangements, or in decisions involving some dilemma, whatever resolution is possible is achieved by finding a "third," or mediator which brings the extremes together into some community. This, according to Royce, is a work of genius, for there is no rule according to which "thirds" are to be discovered.[62] Turning once again to De Morgan, one can find a clear illustration of both the finding of a third and the complex concrete situations and problems for the resolution of which the search is often carried out. The following passage from De Morgan is long but worthy of reproduction in full:

When by the word *syllogism*[63] we agree to mean a composition of two relatives into one, we open the field in such manner that the invention of the middle term, and of the component relations which give the compound relation of the conclusion, is seen to constitute the act of mind which is always occurring in the efforts of the reasoning power. Was an event the consequence of another? We know that consequence of consequence is consequence, and, X being a suspected consequence of Z, we examine various Y's and try if for any one of them we can establish that X is a consequence of Y and Y of Z. . . . The person X, did he commit the act Z? Non-possession of motive is, when taken alone, probable

[61] *The Problem of Christianity*, II, 182.

[62] See M. R. Cohen and E. Nagel, *An Introduction to Logic and Scientific Method*, p. 202, for an excellent statement of this.

[63] It is important to De Morgan's position, if not directly to Royce's that the former regarded the principle of comparison as at the foundation of the syllogism and proposed a *relational* formulation of the principle upon which the syllogism is based. In his symbolism it appears as follows: X . . . L M Z is a consequence of X . . . L Y and Y . . . M Z. He said, "And this is syllogism: it exhibits in the most general form the law of thought which connects two notions by their connections with a third" (*Cambridge Philosophical Transactions*, X, 347).

innocence: non-production of motive is probable non-possession. We try for a motive Y, to which X is related by possession, and Y to Z by sufficiency. Here are the premisses—X is the possessor of the motive Y. Y is a sufficient motive to commit Z; therefore X is the possessor of a sufficient motive to commit Z; and this compound notion is extensively contained in or intensively contains—the relation of "sufficiently in connection with the action to give the evidence of actual commission a claim to consideration under ordinary notions of probability." A very complicated concluding relation; but very familiar in action both to judge, counsel, and jury.[64]

In the light of such an example, Royce's investigation of the motives and results of comparison is more readily to be understood. For Royce the elementary processes of comparison and the more complex processes of interpretation represent, above all, our attempts at unification and the creation of community. Ultimately interpretation aims at self-knowledge through a unification and clarification of both our ideas about ourselves and our ideas about the world of which we are a part. The discursive character of self-knowledge has already been touched on, but it is particularly relevant at this point. Self-understanding on the basis of either perception or conception alone is impossible, according to Royce, because life is too rich and varied and demands the unification of its parts through an interpretation of their meaning which is never provided by perception or conception alone. Unification of what was previously dispersed and fragmentary is achieved precisely through the "third" of comparison and interpretation, and such unification is of the essence of the type of growth characterizing human beings. "Any one," said Royce, "who compares distinct ideas, and discovers a third or mediating idea which interprets the meaning of one in the light of the other, thereby discovers, or invents,[65] a realm of conscious unity which contains the very essence of the life of reason."[66] It is at this juncture that Royce's criticism of Bergson for having overlooked the discursive character of self-knowledge is particularly relevant. Royce maintained that the ideas of instinct and intuition, which

[64] *Cambridge Philosophical Transactions*, X, 355f.
[65] Royce should have decided, for these can scarcely be the same!
[66] *The Problem of Christianity*, II, 188. Cf. *The Sources of Religious Insight*, pp. 89f.

imply a direct and immediate apprehension of life, are inadequate for the characterization of what the artist, the poet, the mathematician, or the statesman are doing when they discover a mediating concept or third that marks some advance in our understanding of ourselves and our world. In such moments of discovery, comparison and interpretation are employed, and an analysis of these processes shows not only that they are discursive, but that what often goes by the term "intuition" is really a process of interpretation. In this criticism of Bergson, Royce's point is well taken, as can easily be shown by appeal to artistic, religious and scientific facts. However, on the other hand, it would be unwise to overlook one element in the view of the defenders of intuition or immediate apprehension which is valuable and for which Royce's analysis provides. The very fact that there is no *rule* according to which "thirds" are to be discovered[67] or hypotheses invented shows that some direct apprehension of the logical connection of ideas is involved in the process of interpretation. The "third" discovered will not indeed in a given case be justified simply on the basis of such direct apprehension, that is, it is not the case that a given interpretation is valid *because* it has been the result in the first instance of a direct apprehension by some mind. Nevertheless, it must be admitted that in the process of interpretation there is some non-discursive element, and that element is the proposal of relevant thirds which are capable of either confirmation or rejection in the course of further experience and interpretation.

Before offering further illustrations of the theory it may be worth while to consider a criticism of Royce's view of interpretation advanced by L. P. Jacks in his review of *The Problem of Christianity:*

Now I can accept all this without serious demur when it is offered as an *ex post facto* description of what *has taken* place when, say, a given scientific discovery has been accomplished. Any attempt to describe that discovery in terms of perception and conception, or the "cashing" of the one into the other, leaves out of account what is most striking in the result of the process, and I can find no objection to the term "inter-

[67] See De Morgan, *A Budget of Paradoxes,* I, 86.

pretation" as supplying what this defective analysis lacks. But if, on the other hand, I am asked to take this account as an adequate rendering from the inside, of what *is taking* place while the mind of the would-be discoverer is engaged in his search, then it seems to me that the essential thing is left out. Professor Royce, unless I misread him, does not observe the distinction between the discover*ing* and the discovery; he does not discriminate between the mind as already possessed of the mediating idea, and the mind while still on the look-out for it. Here are two ideas, A and B, which have to be interpreted one to the other; and C is the mediating idea which will do what is required. I am already in possession of A and B and stand puzzled at their contrast or conflict. I am on the look-out for C. *How do I find it?* A crowd of ideas are offering themselves, in succession or together, as mediators. How from among this throng of candidates do I manage to pick out C as the one which will do the business? By what principle do I reject D, E, F? What are the marks of a genuine mediation? That it mediates? Professor Royce is surely anticipating when he puts "Interpretation" into the cognitive *process* itself. Interpretation is what the process lacks, not what it possesses; and it is precisely as still lacking the interpretation sought, and as still *looking* for it, that knowing, as distinct from knowledge, is a cognitive *function* at all. The particular *functioning* in question is all over when the mediating idea appears. We are told that interpretation is the stimulus and inspiration of knowledge. So in a sense it undoubtedly is. But what is it that inspires the knower while the interpretation is still to seek? These questions may suggest why it seems to me that knowing, as a process in being, escapes the analysis of Professor Royce no less completely than it escapes the analysis of those whom he justly criticizes for reducing it to perception and conception. He has made a finer net than they; but no net however fine will catch the living waters.[68]

Professor Jacks' criticism represents a clear and cogent statement of a real difficulty, and on that account it deserves careful consideration. Certainly no purely logical account of the process of interpretation such as Royce has offered can be taken as a *psychological* account of what presumably takes place in the mind of an actual investigator. However, Royce was well aware that the term interpretation does not refer to the *process* of interpreting but to the "third" or mediating idea which, to use Professor Jacks' language, "will do the business." From the psychological standpoint the interpreter may have to carry on complicated and

[68] *Hibbert Journal*, XII (1913), pp. 219-220.

involved comparisons and imaginings, etc., but the theory of interpretation is not directly concerned with the psychology of the interpreter but with the logical structure of the completed interpretation. Professor Jacks criticized Royce for the failure to distinguish between the mind in possession of the "third" and the one still on the look-out for it, and suggested further that Royce's theory does not tell us how to find the idea which properly constitutes the interpretation. Certainly, as was pointed out above, the logical analysis of the process of interpretation does not provide a set of rules in accordance with which one is enabled to make interpretations. There is no principle on the basis of which one can test the *possible* mediators or "thirds," precisely because testing can only take place after a mediator has been proposed, and as Royce well knew along with Peirce, De Morgan, and countless others acquainted with the history and methods of both empirical investigation and of deduction, the proposal of mediating ideas is guided by no formal rules such as might be formulated for the benefit of inventors and discoverers.[69] De Morgan has made this plain in his papers on the syllogism where he distinguished between the *compound act* of the actual thinker (in syllogism) and the *analyzed compound* of the logician. He said, "It is not true that the law by which thought is governed must be part of the thought which is governed."[70] Yet despite this, the criticism of Professor Jacks is not without importance since it seems clear that Royce, particularly in his criticism of Bergson, regarded interpretation as the form of reason in its living function (particularly when he referred to the "psychology" of interpretation), and it is obvious that he thus laid himself open to the objection that no logical analysis can be

---

[69] See *The Problem of Christianity*, II, 183, where Royce, referring to the act of the interpreter, said, "For this act originality and sometimes even genius may be required." Cf. p. 184. De Morgan, in the section referred to in Note 67, made a similar point in connection with hypotheses and their function: "The trial of the hypothesis is the *special object:* prior to which, hypothesis must have been started, not by rule, but by that sagacity of which no description can be given, precisely because the very owners of it do not act under laws perceptible to themselves."

[70] *Cambridge Philosophical Transactions*, X, 333, note †.

identical with the actual process. In this respect Professor Jacks is correct in saying that "no net however fine will catch the living waters." Nevertheless, it is important to bear in mind the distinction clearly drawn by Royce between the *interpreter*, who makes the comparisons and proposes the mediating ideas, and the ideas themselves, the *interpretations*. The important point for Royce's theory is that interpretation, from either a logical or a psychological standpoint, is not reducible either to perception or to conception alone, since it is neither a "mere" seeing nor a "barren" conceiving.

Two concrete instances may be offered by way of providing some empirical illustration for Royce's theory of interpretation. They are drawn from the fields of biology and of religion. The former concerning Darwin is Royce's own, while the latter is not, but it is clearer than a similar one which he used in his original lecture.[71] Some digression from the strictly philosophical discussion is of course necessitated but the appeal to facts is always of vital importance, since, especially in contemporary philosophy, there is much more talk about the virtues of empirical method and about the nature of an empirical approach than there is straightforward appeal to the available data themselves.

From the science of biology, Royce called attention, by way of illustration, to the work of Darwin and the logical process exhibited in the case of his special interpretation of the hypothesis of evolution. It is well known that Darwin did not propose the idea of evolving natural forms, *de novo*, but that other investigators, including his grandfather Erasmus Darwin and Wallace, had previously accustomed the scientific world to the developmental hypotheses generally known as "evolution." The special contribution of Darwin was his theory of the driving force actuating the movement, and of the principle according to which the movement is to be rendered intelligible. His own observations together with those of previous investigators had definitely established the fact of variation both as individual differences and as strongly marked deviations of structure. It remained for Darwin to propose a hypothesis explaining the survival of some indi-

[71] See *The Problem of Christianity*, II, 190f.

viduals and the disappearance of others. Obviously what was needed, to use Royce's language, was a "third" or mediating idea which could stand between the facts of individual variation and survival. In *The Descent of Man*,[72] Darwin mentioned his reading of Malthus' *Essay on the Principle of Population* in which it was shown that population tends to increase beyond the subsistence level (a level relative to the natural and artificial conditions of the given region). The result is a natural checking of the increase through the situation of overcrowding which follows. This principle of Malthus' provided the mediating idea for Darwin. He wrote:

> The early progenitors of man must also have tended, like all other animals, to have increased beyond their means of subsistence; they must, therefore, occasionally have been exposed to a struggle for existence, and consequently to the rigid law of natural selection. Beneficial variations of all kinds will thus, either occasionally or habitually, have been preserved and injurious ones eliminated.[73]

By means of the mediating idea the fact of variation was interpreted to the fact of survival, and the process of evolution was thereby viewed as a natural development in which "beneficial" variations lead to survival and "injurious" ones are eliminated.[74]

A situation may be taken from the history of religion to illustrate the function of comparison and interpretation, which is both impressive in itself and striking because of the precision with which the logic of the situation is revealed in it. In chapters 40–55 of the Old Testament book of the prophet Isaiah[75] (generally known to scholars and critics in these matters as the "second" or "deutero" Isaiah), there is a record of one of the most exalted insights to be found in any religious tradition. If

---

[72] *The Descent of Man* (Modern Library Ed.), pp. 428ff.

[73] *Ibid.*, p. 431.

[74] No complete or even adequate statement of Darwin's position is intended. It is sufficient for this discussion that the function of the mediating idea be pointed out.

[75] Royce's own illustration was from the experience of the prophet Amos. Such an example would do well enough, but it is not as clear as the one in the text. See *The Problem of Christianity*, II, 190.

the date assigned to these chapters by critics is correct, the situation is post-exilic (that is, after 586 B.C.), and the center of attention is Israel's[76] punishment at the hands of Jahweh. The writer of these chapters has presented the results of what, from the standpoint of the preceding analyses, would have to be viewed as a process of comparison and interpretation. The situation has two aspects each one of which exhibits the same logical process, but since they supplement each other and provide a completed picture of the "second Isaiah's" prophecy, it is wise to present both as follows:

1. The first contrast, or pair of conflicting ideas, which confronted the prophet was the antithesis between Jahweh's law, which is righteousness and truth and which stands at the basis of the covenant (*berith*) between Jahweh and his people, on the one hand, and the actual apostasy of the people,[77] on the other. The prophetic idea of punishment at the hands of Jahweh interprets the situation of exile. According to the prophet, the suffering of exile is the punishment which ensues when a rift between Israel and her God appears as a result of the people's having turned away from him:

Who gave Jacob for a spoil, and Israel to the robbers? did not Jehovah? he against whom we have sinned, and in whose ways they would not walk, neither were they obedient unto his law. Therefore he poured upon him the fierceness of his anger, and the strength of battle (42: 24-25a, ARV).

The above passage follows directly upon passages in which Jahweh's righteousness and power have been emphasized. The "therefore" in the text shows that the prophet regarded the actual historical situation of exile as a punishment resulting from the antithesis previously noted—

Behold, I have refined thee, but not as silver; I have tried thee in the furnace of affliction (48:10 mg., ARV).

[76] "Israel" is used here to denote the whole nation, not the north as distinct from the south or Judah.

[77] This first contrast is characteristic of the book of "first Isaiah" (1-39) throughout. See, for example, 6:5.

The present reality is *interpreted* by the prophet as punishment following upon the contrast between perfect righteousness and that state of separation from Jahweh in which the people existed prior to the fall of Jerusalem. The idea of punishment interprets the contrast and makes meaningful the suffering.

2. Having made one comparison and interpretation the prophet faced a second, and in some ways more complex, contrast— the antithesis between the dignity of the nation as Jahweh's people, on the one hand, and the terrible treatment Israel had received at the hands of both the Assyrians and the Babylonians, on the other. Israel appeared to have suffered perhaps even more than her share:

> Comfort ye, comfort ye my people saith your God. Speak ye to the heart of Jerusalem; and cry unto her that her punishment is accepted, that her iniquity is pardoned, that she hath received of Jehovah's hand double for all her sins (4:1-2 mg., ARV).

In the light of the contrast between the special position of Israel and her "unclean" and boastful conquerors, the prophet sought to give a further interpretation of the punishment involved. The idea of the "suffering servant," first advanced by this prophet, however it may be interpreted in its details by critics,[78] represents one of the finest illustrations of interpretation to be found anywhere in religious literature. That Israel suffers not only to be purified and restored to Jahweh again, but that through her suffering the presence and the saving power of Jahweh may become known to the Gentiles (that is, $\tau \grave{a}$ $E\theta \nu a$, the nations), is the "third" which interprets the contrast between Israel the downtrodden, oppressed by blasphemers and idolaters, and Israel the people of Jahweh.

The function of the prophet in any religious situation is revelatory in character. If the triadic structure may be employed

---

[78] Perhaps no idea in the Old Testament has been the occasion of more discussion and variety of interpretation than this one. See R. H. Pfeiffer, *Introduction to the Old Testament*, pp. 459ff., for concrete details. For the purpose of this discussion the precise meaning of the idea and how it may finally be interpreted is not as important as its function as a third or interpretant.

here, it is obvious that the prophet stands between Jahweh and his people and says, in effect, What Jahweh says is what I say. This is consistently and clearly illustrated in the typical expression of the great tradition of Hebrew prophecy, "Thus saith the Lord . . ." The prophet then is the one who interprets the divine mind to the religious community through the signs of that mind which appear in history.[79]

Turning to the motives of comparison and interpretation, Royce maintained that the will to be self-possessed, to be guided by genuine insight independent of whim or fancy, is fundamental. It may appear, he said, as if comparison could provide only the most meager and momentary knowledge, since it is dependent on such variable factors as individual experience, the power of discernment possessed by the particular interpreter, etc., and that consequently it is of small significance to either philosophy or religion. Royce, however, did not believe this to be the case because, in the process of deduction, which is precisely the process of finding "thirds," when a consequence is reached, a fact of some significance has been discovered. This fact is, not that the conclusion is true (although it may be), but that the conclusion "follows from" the premises. He considered the discovery of such logical connection and implications to be the uncovering of what is both highly important and very precise, even though the concrete situation within which such interpretation takes place may appear to be such as to yield only momentary and insignificant truth.[80] It is crucial for Royce's theory that the discovery of what it is that "follows from" the premises in question involves a process which is not reducible either to perception or to conception, but rather it is a process of interpretation.

The charge that deduction never yields *novel conclusions* and hence teaches nothing not already known—a difficulty which can not be treated fully here—may be answered, as Royce correctly noted, by the counter-assertion that the consequences, that is,

[79] It is history which is the specific medium of "revelation" in the Old Testament. See C. H. Cornill, *The Prophets of Israel*, p. 11. *Cf.* Spinoza, *A Theologico-Political Treatise*, Ch. I, for a clear statement of the prophet as interpreter.

[80] See Peirce, *Collected Papers*, I, 66.

what "follows from" or is "implied by" a given set of premises, are myriad in number as compared with the premises from which one begins, as can be shown by any system of geometry. It would be a rash individual who would be prepared to assert that the consequences of a given set of assumptions are known at the outset just as the definitions, postulates, and rules of inference are known. This means that the above charge is unwarranted because what is "new" in a deductive system is just those propositions that are implied by the premises which, although "contained in" (because "implied by") the premises, must still be discovered. The enterprise of understanding both man and the world is precisely the problem of discovering the consequences of what is already known, and then using these consequences in turn as premises from which still more numerous consequences may be discovered to follow.

Royce further extended the meaning of comparison, and the insight involved, to refer to the mastery over life gained by the individual who succeeds in understanding the world and his place in it.[81] Royce referred to the insights thus gained as the attainment of a vision broader than and beyond the fragmentariness of our separate and contrasting ideas, and it is just at this point that he came closest to the Hegelian type of rationalism. For example, comparison can reach truth, because "we are wider than any of our ideas,"[82] and consequently antitheses and oppositions are "overcome," that is, unified by the discovery of a "third," through a vision wide enough to embrace the contrasting ideas involved. This is very close indeed to the Hegelian higher synthesis. It must not be overlooked, however, that Royce generally used the term "insight,"[83] referring to what the Platonic tradition has called "wisdom." This is not identical with that absolute knowledge which Hegel considered capable of attaining the absolute unity and which is the goal of all knowing, because

[81] See *The Problem of Christianity*, II, 203.

[82] *Loc. cit.*

[83] See *The Sources of Religious Insight*, p. 5, where Royce said that insight is the name for a type of knowledge involving acquaintance as well as descriptive capacity.

of the element of immediacy ("acquaintance") which such insight or wisdom contains.

In passing from individual self-knowledge to the interpretation of many selves, Royce maintained once again that the psychology of such interpretation is identical with the process of comparison. The interpreter C, according to him, is in possession of certain signs which are significative of A's mind and of certain signs significative of B's mind. The only difference between social and individual interpretation is the degree of clarity which is possible. In self-interpretation a degree of clarity is attained by the interpreter which is never possible for that same interpreter in his attempt to interpret other minds.[84] Thus individual selves are differentiated, in Leibnizian fashion, according to the degree of clarity attained in the process of interpretation.

It is necessary at this point to consider more fully what Royce referred to as the motives underlying the process of interpretation. He never lost sight of these and this is what constitutes his pragmatism or, if Dewey is correct, his voluntarism. The three terms involved in interpretation appear as three selves between which there exist certain chasms. The will to interpret, according to Royce, is the will to cross these boundaries, to bridge these chasms, and create community where none existed before. He proposed the following analysis:[85]

1. I, as prospective interpreter, am aware of a neighbor as a set of "leadings," meanings, pursuits and purposes into which I have not the clearest insight.

2. My own narrowness of insight and the separation of the other from me moves me to pass beyond this state and create a community.

3. The will to interpret expresses itself in the attempt to interpret one of my neighbors to another of my neighbors.

4. C, the interpreter, if the enterprise be successful, will

[84] Royce conceded a point to the intuitionists here, for he suggested that in self-interpretation the self in question stands in a privileged position, so to speak, in the process of interpreting its own signs, which presumably would not be the case if self-knowledge were *wholly discursive*.

[85] *The Problem of Christianity*, II, 210ff.

possess a vision of A's ideas, of his own, and of B's, and the result will be a spiritual unity between the three, although as Royce noted, this implies no mystic blending of the selves in which individuality is lost, for the terms of the triadic relation must remain *distinct*. If A is *willing* to be interpreted by C, and B is *willing* to have A interpreted to him, and both are *willing* to have C as an interpreter, then these three constitute a *community of interpretation* possessing a definite form. The goal of completed interpretation which would bring all selves into community is, like the completion of truth, never realized in any finite time, but the goal is no less real for Royce on that account. Royce formulated this envisaged goal of the will to interpret in the following terms:

> Our individual experience of our successful comparisons of our own ideas shows us wherein it (the goal of interpretation) consists, and that it is no goal which an abstract conception can define in terms of credit values, and that it is also no goal which a possible perception can render to me in the cash of any set of sensory data. Yet it is a goal which each of us can accept as his own. I can at present aim to approach that goal through plans, through hypotheses regarding you which can be inductively tested. I can view that goal as a common future event. We can agree upon that goal. And, herewith I interpret not only you as the being whom I am to interpret, but also myself as in ideal the interpreter who aims to approach the vision of the unity of precisely this community. And you, and my other neighbor to whom I address my interpretation, can also interpret yourselves accordingly.[86]

The end or goal of interpretation for Royce is always the "practical" one of creating community where none existed before. Thus the true lover of mankind can do nothing more significant for mankind than the fostering of the will to interpret "somebody to somebody" through the creation of communities of interpretation. All social enterprises embody this will, he said, and although they may be as widely different in character and in aim as can be imagined, they all exhibit the same triadic logical structure which alone makes possible an understanding of both

[86] *Ibid.*, II, 212.

life and world and thereby overcomes the separations between selves which are rooted in such divisive factors as ignorance, pride, fear and distrust. Royce regarded the community conception, involving the interpreter, as it does, as definitive of the nature of reality. "And if," he said, "in ideal, we aim to conceive the divine nature, how better can we conceive it than in the form of the *Community of Interpretation*, and above all, in the form of the Interpreter, who interprets all to all, and each individual to the world, and the world of spirits to each individual."[87] The whole of reality then is a vast system in which the present interprets the past to the future. The system is infinite in character precisely because all interpretations are themselves signs which will stand in need of further interpretation in the future. Further interpretation can be offered as long as the community exists unbroken and continues the process of interpretation. The completion of such a process is real for the ideal interpreter since he is the one, so to speak, who possesses the interpretation not itself in need of further interpretation—that is, the absolute truth. Hence the infinite is actual as the infinity of minds in community, as the interpreter or spirit, and as final or complete interpretation which is absolute truth.

Before turning from the general analysis of the community of interpretation to the special instance of community with which

---

[87] *Ibid.*, II, 219. (Italics not in original.) Although the issue of theism and pantheism in Royce should perhaps be dealt with more fully, since it is not of vital importance to this discussion it has been left to a footnote. Miss Calkins and others carried on a lively discussion with Royce concerning his pantheism which Miss Calkins particularly thought was not in harmony with Christian theism. (See *Papers in Honor of Josiah Royce*, pp. 54-56, where the attempt is made to show the harmony between Royce and theism.) Actually Royce, like the Trinitarian theology, attempted to combine both poles of Christian thought in his doctrine. Christian theology has oscillated, in its history, between theism and pantheism in emphasis. The Trinitarian doctrine represents an attempt to reconcile these conceptions. Royce is close, I believe, to a Trinitarian view, precisely because God is equally the community, the Absolute and the interpreter (that is, Spirit, Father, Son). This is obvious both from the passage quoted above in the text and from Royce's statement that the *terms* of the community of interpretation are interchangeable although the *relations* between them remain the same. Professor Boas has some wise remarks on the whole discussion in his article "The History of Philosophy," in *Naturalism and the Human Spirit*, pp. 134f.

this study is concerned, the Beloved Community, or the church, it is necessary to set forth what it is that Royce referred to as the "problem of Christianity." This is of the greatest importance because his community metaphysic, as will be apparent, provides the basis for whatever solution to this problem is possible. The following chapter will be concerned with the task of setting forth the "problem," and the succeeding one will deal with the Beloved Community as well as certain of the Christian ideas connected with it.

CHAPTER FOUR

THE PROBLEM OF CHRISTIANITY

George Santayana, who easily surpasses all philosophers in the charm with which he says things that are patently false, ventured to say of Royce, "His reward was that he became a prophet to a whole class of earnest, troubled people who, having discarded doctrinal religion, wished to think their life worth living when, to look at what it contained, it might not have seemed so."[1] What is germane in the above to the theme of this discussion is the reference to those "having discarded doctrinal religion." It is not difficult to see how one might come to this erroneous conclusion about Royce's religious thought, especially if the lectures entitled *The World and the Individual* and the fact that Royce is an idealist were the only facts about him one had in mind. Doubtless Santayana had never read *The Problem of Christianity* or he never would have been led to make such a remark The mere fact that the "problem" of the Christian religion is in Royce's view a consequence of certain intellectual difficulties attached to the Christian *ideas* or *dogmas* shows that Royce adopted no moralistic or purely "spiritual" interpretation of Christianity.[2] Royce can be shown to be in accord with doctrinal Christianity, as embodied in the great Christian thinkers, because he never really lost sight of the fact that Christianity offers an interpretation of existence, that is, that it contains a metaphysics, and that it is not merely an ethics.

From the outset, Royce was definite in his judgment that

[1] G. Santayana, *Character and Opinion in the United States*, p. 119. See a review by E. S. Carr in *Bibliotheca Sacra*, LXXI (1914), pp. 283ff., where it is noted that certain Calvinist circles regarded Royce as their champion and a defender of the faith!

[2] The criticism of Harnack's position advanced by Royce should be ample proof of this. See *The Problem of Christianity*, I, xxivff.

the *social* character of Christianity is its essential character, and he repeatedly called attention to his agreement with Pauline thought on this point.[3] The church[4] represents the central reality because it is only in the corporate body that the spirit of loyalty can appear. Consequently Royce was particularly critical of James's basic approach in *The Varieties of Religious Experience*, where the latter confined his attention to individual and purely personal experience, at the same time suggesting that the social expression of religion in the church must always be conventional and hence secondary in importance.[5] All religious experience, Royce admitted, is at least individual, that is, it is always the experience of someone, but to so restrict it, he added, is hopelessly inadequate, for the fullest and richest human experience is social in character as is shown in this particular sphere by the omnipresence in all cultures of the religious *community*. Royce believed himself in accord with the Pauline view when he maintained that the essence of Christianity is the community, and further that the beloved community is the rock upon which the church is built. Since the salvation of the individual is the ultimate aim of the Christian religion, it would follow that the Christian community is intimately bound up with the process of redemption. This is precisely Royce's view—that is, that ultimately the beloved community is what redeems the individual; and it is the central task of *The Problem of Christianity* to offer both a careful analysis of the communities of interpretation and a metaphysical defense of the ultimate reality of the actual infinite, of God, and his redeeming power actual in the beloved community.

Royce, as a student of both the history and philosophy of religion, was well aware of a central concern of all thoughtful adherents of a religious tradition: the problem of clarifying the

[3] The relation of Pauline Christianity to Royce's interpretation of the Christian ideas will be discussed below.

[4] Actually it is the beloved community and not any historical church which is the ultimate spiritual reality for Royce.

[5] No direct reference is given, but Royce no doubt referred to Lecture II of the *Varieties* (Modern Library Edition, pp. 30f.), in which James renounced all concern with "institutional" religion, because of his interest in individual religious experience.

basic religious insights of the tradition through more extended knowledge and wider experience, and also of interpreting those insights in the intellectual and moral terms and categories which are best understood by the people of a given time. Royce knew that the perennial "problem" of Christianity is that of achieving some intelligible synthesis between its basic insights and the whole body of "secular" thought and culture in which the Christian community finds itself at a given time. One may even say, and not without sound historical justification, that the entire enterprise of theology in the Christian tradition has been an attempt to cast the "wisdom of God" in the form of the "wisdom of this world," and that Christian theology has encountered or become a "problem" whenever the churches have simply taken over the theological formulations of previous periods without endeavoring to restate such theology by making use of whatever new discoveries, concepts, and methods have appeared in the meantime.

Taking up the position of one who, as philosopher, is neither an apologist for Christianity nor its avowedly hostile critic, Royce proceeded to point out that to those for whom Christianity is neither fully accepted, on the one hand, nor totally rejected, on the other, it becomes a problem. The awareness on the part of the keen observer of those difficulties both practical and theoretical which are attached to the Christian world view make it imperative that someone who is neither an apologist in the strict sense[6] nor a hostile critic in any sense you please, should take up the task of interpretation, for only such a one is able to be an interpreter.

An illustration of how the interpreter would function, according to Royce's theory, in a concrete situation of this kind will be helpful at this point. As interpreter (B), he stands between the apologist (A), and the hostile critic or assailant (C) as follows:

A. Apologist

B. Interpreter

C. Assailant

[6] In a sense which would apply to such thinkers as Clement of Alexandria, Origen, etc.

The interpreter can perform the following two distinct functions (although the *logical* structure of the process remains the same in both cases):

1. He can say to A that when C says such and such he is saying what I say to you. Conversely, to C, he says that when A says such and such he is saying what I say to you. Depending on the skill of the interpreter and the *willingness* of A and C to *understand* each other, even if they cannot *agree*, some understanding of what A is talking about may be gained by C and *vice versa*. This function is of vital importance at the present time in all questions of philosophical or theological import, for it is possible that through such interpretation thinkers holding opposed positions may gain an understanding of each other's positions which would not be possible if each were to insist on regarding as meaningful only what satisfies his own conditions for meaningful discourse. One illustration of this must suffice. If the question, "Why do men die?" is put, it would be understood by some to be meaningful only if it could be answered by asserting a proposition (p) appearing in one of the specific sciences which is warranted by whatever evidence is judged relevant for such warrant. Obviously if the original question is *only* meaningful in that sense, then the one to whom it means the asking of a religious or metaphysical question of the form, "Why is it the case that p is the case?" where this precludes, in principle, an answer in the form of another proposition (q) occurring in a science from which propositions in the science in which (p) occurs may validly be deduced, would seem to be asking a "meaningless" question. A sympathetic interpreter might induce the parties in question to *understand* what it is that the other party has in mind, although they may not be able to *agree* with each other in the sense that certain crucial propositions could be accepted as the truth of the matter by both sides. Such interpretation if it did not (as it probably could not) produce agreement, would at least create community and that is indeed something not to be regarded lightly at the present time.

2. The interpreter can say to C that when A says such and such, he is expressing in his language the same thought which you express when you say such and such, and conversely to A about C. This distinct, but closely allied, function of the interpreter enables workers in various fields and persons of different backgrounds and experiences to discover the instances in which they are talking about the same thing as someone else although they may never have been aware of this before. One illustration must suffice again. When, for example, the modern philosophic naturalist rejects the validity of propositions of the form "A is *nothing but* B," thereby expressing a rejection of the dogmatism which would totally identify A, some subject standing in an infinite number of relations as a part of the natural world, with just one of its features B, he is saying in his language what Christianity expresses when it, following its Platonic heritage, says that no item of finite truth should be taken unconditionally as if it were truth itself, or as Whitehead has expressed the idea, "finitude is not self-supporting."[7] Again, the discovery that what was formerly either regarded as separated or not regarded at all is really unified, constitutes the work of interpretation and results in the establishing of community through the efforts of the interpreter. It should be apparent that the interpreter is one basically committed to a belief in the unity of the world.[8]

Having noted these functions of interpretation, it is necessary to return to the main theme in order to indicate in greater detail just what the "problem" of Christianity is. It was hinted above that the problem centers about a conflict, and now that conflict can be stated explicitly. Each contemporary person, according to Royce, may be regarded as the heir to the "education of the human race" in so far as he possesses both the recorded experience and the knowledge of his predecessors as well as that of his own

[7] A. N. Whitehead, "Mathematics and the Good," in *The Library of Living Philosophers*, p. 670. See F. H. Bradley, *Essays on Truth and Reality*, p. 323, for the same idea.
[8] See *The Problem of Christianity*, I, 12ff.

time. On the other hand, he is also heir to a great religious tradition containing a fully articulated view of nature, man, God, and the relations obtaining between them. Unfortunately for him, this religious tradition as formulated is not easily intelligible in terms of his intellectual heritage and even appears, on many points, to be flatly mistaken because in direct conflict with that heritage. The problem of Christianity is, as ˉRoyce formulated it, "In what sense, if in any, can the modern man consistently be, in creed,[9] a Christian?"[10] Or as Royce put it in still another way, how do the Christian ideas meet the test of being judged in terms of the wisdom of the human race? The successful interpretation of one tradition to the other would constitute, for Royce, the solution of the problem.

What is of the utmost importance for an understanding of the problem from which he set out is the stress Royce placed on the interpretative or theological aspect of Christianity. In one place[11] he suggested that if one is content with the view that Christianity is in essence wholly practical, that is, that it is an ethic and nothing more, then there would be no problem of Christianity (precisely because the issue at stake would be completely overlooked) for such an individual. But Royce was prepared to go to the root of the matter by raising the question of the grounds upon which the modern man may still regard as justified the world view offered by Christianity, and this is indeed to pass beyond the confines of ethics.[12] Royce formulated the problem in still another way which is perhaps the most adequate:

When we consider what are the essential features of Christianity, is the acceptance of a creed that embodies these features consistent with the lessons that, so far as we can yet learn, the growth of human wisdom and the course of the ages have taught man regarding religious truth?[13]

[9] By "in creed" Royce meant that he is to maintain the *interpretation* of existence offered by Christianity, not only the ethics.

[10] *Ibid.*, I, 14.

[11] *Ibid.*, I, 24-25.

[12] It is just this failure to take note of Royce's interest in Christian theology that vitiates Santayana's view of Royce.

[13] *Ibid.*, I, 21.

The enterprise which Royce set for himself in the lectures which are the main consideration of this discussion follows directly from this statement of his problem. Royce proposed, first, to set forth his view of the essence of Christianity, and, secondly, to examine the relation in which these essential Christian ideas stand both to the lessons of history and to the truth about life and the world (what Royce referred to as the "real world"). In order to point out the link between this enterprise and the discussion of the preceding chapters, it is sufficient to say that, for Royce, Christianity is concentrated in the doctrine of the Beloved Community and that the problem of Christianity will be, in some sense, solved if the nature and function of that community can be shown to be consistent with both man's moral and religious experience and the metaphysic implied therein. To state this more simply, the successful completion of Royce's discussion means showing that the real world is of the nature of a community and hence that the Christian doctrine of the Beloved Community is both in harmony with that view of the world and intelligible in its terms.

It should be borne in mind at the outset that anyone who proposes to state the essence of Christianity faces an extremely difficult task. Contrary to the popular opinion that religious controversies, particularly doctrinal ones, are artificial and represent hair-splitting and that they can easily be avoided by a return to "simple" Christianity or the like, the task of setting forth the essence of Christianity is a tremendous one. No further proof is needed of the difficulty involved than the history of the Roman Church itself. Certainly no other branch of Christianity has attempted to define so carefully and with such awesome rigor the essence of the faith, and yet Roman Christianity has, in the course of its history, added to the content of "revelation" much that is foreign both to the religion of the New Testament community and to the mind of Christ[14] (in so far, that is, as this

[14] Many illustrations might be offered here, if space permitted. It is sufficient to point out that the very fact that Thomas Aquinas thought it necessary to maintain the doctrine that no "new" propositions are added to Christian truth which are not *implicit* in the original deposit of faith to Peter, shows that the

can be assumed to be an actual possession within definable limits). It can be said with confidence that if the Roman Church, the institution always claiming absolute and reliable authority for Christianity, has encountered difficulty in defining the faith and has maintained at one time what was obviously not maintained at another, then in the light of this, the difficulty of stating the necessary and vital Christian affirmations will be apparent. Actually, what is regarded as the core of Christianity will be determined, in a given case, by the answer to the prior question: Upon what grounds will the issue be decided? Royce, standing as he did in the Protestant tradition, decided that the New Testament community established as the Church, its experience and its life, should be normative in any discussion of the essence of Christianity.

Royce included among the principal features of Christianity, first, that it was taught and lived out by a concrete person who served as an example to his followers, and, second, that it involved an *interpretation* by his followers of the Master's mission. Concerning the second feature, Royce said, in words particularly pertinent to present discussions of these matters:

> Historically speaking, Christianity has never appeared simply as the religion taught by the Master. It has always been an interpretation of the Master and of his religion in the light of some doctrine concerning his mission, and also concerning God, Man, and Man's Salvation,—a doctrine which, even in its simplest expressions, has always gone beyond what the Master himself is traditionally reported to have taught while he lived.[15]

It is impossible, as becomes increasingly apparent after a century of pure historicism, to ignore the second of these features through any reduction of Christianity to the "real" religion or ethic of Jesus. On this head, Royce was on sound ground. Moreover, the distinction, as he rightly noted, between the Master and some interpretation of his significance is certainly not a

---

adoption of new and foreign ideas in the Roman tradition stood in need of justification. See *Summa Theol.* II (ii), Qu. 1. a. 8.

[15] *Ibid.*, I, 25.

modern invention. Nor is it one introduced by those who are
often accused of interpreting Christianity after their own private
views. Not only has it been the subject of much (often bitter)
discussion in the history of the church,[16] but it is contained
within both the New Testament and the earliest Christian literature. Royce further believed, and there is also good warrant
for this, that the significance of Jesus' earthly life is not itself
apprehensible without appeal to what was evident to his followers
only after his death. If this is true, then Christianity is certainly
more than the religion taught by Jesus in the sayings and parables.

What Royce intended, by fixing the distinction (not necessarily
the separation) between what he later called the historical and
the essential, is clear. He did not believe that a picture of Christianity as nothing but a religion embodying a way of life exemplified
by the historical founder and contained in his sayings is true to
its essence, nor did he believe that a purely practical solution to the
problem of Christianity would suffice. Hence he emphasized the
interpretative or theological aspect of Christianity, because he
believed that the "problem" centers there. In this respect Royce
was correct. The attempt on the part of the believers of Christian
faith to reduce it to an ethic, in order to meet contemporary
criticism, has certainly not been successful, precisely because it
is the Christian world view that most often seems the stumbling
block to the modern man, and the Christian ethic is itself definitely
rooted in that world view, that is, in more general assumptions
concerning the nature of man, his relation to God, and his destiny.
The neglect of this last aspect has greatly contributed to the
weakness of the purely ethical conception of the Christian faith.
Royce saw this in his own time, and what he saw then is all the
more pertinent at present, because, since the second decade of this
century, Christian thought has moved full circle, and is again
attempting to take seriously the full Christian tradition which
embodies religious and theological elements as well as its ethics.

Of the two features of Christianity singled out above, Royce

[16] For example, the Arian controversy concerns, among other things, the
distinction between Jesus as historical example and as Saviour in some religious
and theological sense.

placed the emphasis, as might be expected, on the side of interpretation. He offered no detailed justification for his view at the outset, except a few suggestions which are themselves not without merit. Royce pointed to the fact that certain remarks Jesus is reported to have made about love, the kingdom, self-sacrifice, etc., were not only dimly understood by his disciples, but have remained to a high degree incomprehensible ever since.[17] The earliest Christian communities, according to Royce, guided by the apostle Paul, dwelt on these points and offered an interpretation which they believed was guided by the Lord's spirit.[18] For this reason Royce believed that these interpretations which grew out of the life and thought of the early communities are of the first importance for an understanding of the core of the Christian religion. It is not that he regarded these interpretations as a body of ideas *de novo* simply set forth by the community, but that he believed the community was first aware of the implications of Jesus' teaching and his mission, and, consequently, that it came to articulate these implications in a form capable of being shared. Royce further maintained, in order to refute the charge that, on his view, Paul or the Church had initiated Christianity and not Jesus,[19] that the new community always thought itself in essential harmony with, and dependent upon, the beliefs and the spirit of Jesus, as is obvious both from Paul's conviction about possessing the mind of Christ, and the belief expressed in the Fourth Gospel[20] in the continuing spirit which leads unto all truth. In Royce's terms, the Spirit assumes the office of interpreter making possible the knowledge of things new though in essential harmony with (because implied by) things old.

Before continuing the discussion it is of the first importance that something be said concerning the point mentioned in the above paragraph, one of the most controversial in Royce's inter-

[17] It must be borne in mind that no problem of interpretation exists for Christianity if, for example, an infallible church by definition knows what God meant at each point. On such a basis there is no problem (and no solution either).

[18] John 16:13 refers to what Royce had in mind.

[19] See an interesting remark on this head by Kant in *Religion Within the Limits of Reason Alone*, pp. 139f.

[20] For example, John 15:26.

pretation of Christianity: whether the historical founder of Christianity is neglected and replaced by the community in his view. That this was a subject of much discussion in Royce's time is a matter of historical fact, and there is little reason to believe that it would cease to be important at present were Royce to be re-examined. A good case can be made for the view that Royce did not overlook the historical person, Jesus, but before offering any defense it seems worthwhile to set forth and examine briefly some of the criticisms which have been put forward on this point. One writer, equipped with more sarcasm than understanding, has made the following statement:

> Royce asserts emphatically and a little peevishly in the Preface [*The Problem of Christianity*] that he has never been an Hegelian, and that if he has been he has reformed. It is a little hard to make this square with his attitude towards the individual founder of the church. The cavalier treatment accorded the individual over against the community seems in exact harmony with the general Hegelian theory, where the individual is always getting lost in the void of the pantheistic Absolute.[21]

Although it is not altogether clear what the "cavalier treatment" of the individual refers to here, the writer seems to be echoing a well-known criticism against Hegel and simply assuming that it must apply to Royce as well. Further consideration of this criticism is not necessary; but such is not the case with the two succeeding critics. William Adams Brown, whose review of Royce's lectures[22] is most careful and well-informed, also criticized him for neglecting the founder of Christianity, and he referred to a statement of Royce's[23] that there is never "any human and visible triumph of the ideal in history," in support of his contention. W. E. Hocking, in his discerning review of *The Problem of Christianity*, makes a similar criticism by calling attention to what he takes to be Royce's neglect of the historical foundations of Christianity and particularly of the doctrine of the Incarnation. Professor Hocking's remarks are instructive on the point, as the following passage will show:

[21] *Bibliotheca Sacra* (1914), pp. 292f.
[22] *Journal of Philosophy*, XI (1914), pp. 608-616.
[23] *The Problem of Christianity*, II, 430.

Neither the atoning deed nor the divine community is brought to earth by this doctrine in historically identifiable form, valid for all men as a common object. Christianity is left in the region of the universal; and thereby the foundation for a truly universal community, an historic unity of all particular spirits and their loyal endeavors, is not laid. If this is true, it may be because that one of all the characteristic ideas of Christianity which to many thinkers is most central has retreated into the background and at last eluded our author's grasp—the doctrine of the Incarnation.[24]

The criticisms by the preceding two writers may be taken as typical statements of a difficulty which Royce's theory must meet. Both are dissatisfied with Royce's interpretation of Christianity, for it is alleged (a) to have neglected the concrete individual, the historical Jesus, and (b) to have provided no real foundation in history for the Christian religion and particularly for the church. It now remains to consider these objections by reference to Royce's own statements.

The passage cited by Brown is an unfortunate one, because Royce was referring there not to Jesus but to the development of the beloved community, and he was maintaining, in accordance with both Old and New Testament tradition, that the completion of that community (God as "all in all") does not occur as an event besides other events in history, but rather that it is the goal of all history. Hence it is hardly accurate to use this passage in support of the contention that for Royce the ideal never appears in history. What is overlooked by Brown, and this applies to Hocking's criticism as well, is that the person and the deed which make the beloved community possible in the first instance are a person and a deed which appear in history, for Royce. For him, the course of history is the growth to completion of the saving community, and as such this perfection is never reached at any historical period, but the conditions making that community possible in the first instance are actual indeed and actual as historical. The following passages from *The Problem of Christianity* will illustrate this contention:

    1. Paul and his apostolic Christians were not content with family

[24] *Harvard Theological Review*, VII (1914), p. 112.

loyalty, or with clan loyalty, or with a love for any community that they conceived as merely natural in its origin. A miracle, as they held, had created the body of Christ (I, 170).

2. For the new life of loyalty, if it appears at all, will arise as a bond linking many highly self-conscious and mutually estranged social individuals in one; but this bond can come to mean anything living and real to these individuals, only in case some potent and loyal individual, acting as leader, first declares that for him it is real. In such a leader, and in his spirit, the community will begin its own life, if the leader has the power to create what he loves.

The individual who initiates this process will then plausibly appear to an onlooker, such as Paul was when he was converted, to be at once an individual and the spirit—the very life—of a community. But his origin will be inexplicable in terms of the processes which he himself originated. His power will come from another level than our own. And of the workings of this grace, when it has appeared, we can chiefly say this: That such love is propagated by personal example, although how, we cannot explain (I, 185-186).

3. We know how Paul conceives the beginning of the new life wherein Christian salvation is to be found. This beginning he refers to the work of Christ. The Master was an individual man. To Paul's mind, his mission was divine. He both knew and loved his community before it existed on earth; for his foreknowledge was one with that of the God whose will he came to accomplish. On earth he called into this community its first members. He suffered and died that it might have life. Through his death and in his life the community lives. *He is now identical with the spirit of this community*. This, according to Paul, was the divine grace which began the process of salvation for man (I, 186-187).

The above quotations are lengthy but it is necessary to be clear concerning Royce's view of the difficult matter in question. The preceding charges that Royce has neglected the historical Jesus and that he has no foundation in history for the church must be judged to be mistaken in the light of the above sections from *The Problem of Christianity*. From (a) it is clear that Royce took the beloved community as a community which does not arise in the "natural" way of such units of loyalty as the family, nation, etc. The body of Christ, or that community which alone is the saving community, has as a necessary condition of its existence some event to which Royce referred as a "miracle."

From (b) it is clear that this "miracle" is the appearance of the individual whose life, work, and death make possible the establishing of the divine community, and that, apart from the appearance of such an individual possessing the power to create such a reality, there would be no community at all. From this passage it is also clear that the individual in question serves as an example to his followers. From (c) it is evident that Royce, following the faith of Paul, regarded Jesus as an individual man through whom the divine grace is manifest precisely in so far as he initiates the community which redeems.[25]

If it be objected, and this is what Hocking seems to have in mind when he makes his criticism in reference to the Incarnation, that on Royce's view salvation is not accomplished "at an instant," because God or the ideal personality does not appear in his fulness in history but only as the initiator of "the process of salvation for men,"[26] then the answer is that any interpretation of Christianity in which salvation for all men throughout all time is already a matter of fact, in virtue of the appearance of the Christ, must be unsatisfactory, because it renders the course of history meaningless. Royce was prepared to say, with Paul, that the divine has indeed appeared and made the atoning deed[27] which renders possible the reconciliation of God and man, and also that such reconciliation is itself a process the fulfilment of which is the completion of the beloved community. Royce is in accord with Paul, who maintained that the divine had indeed appeared in all fulness, but that the ultimate reconciliation between God and man (what Paul refers to as God being "all in all") is realized only when all men have been subject to the Christ who is himself subject to God.[28] It is difficult to see how Royce can be criticized for having neglected historical foundations, as Hocking has objected, precisely because for him the beloved community is established in history by an event

[25] See, in addition to the above passages, *The Problem of Christianity*, I, 192.

[26] *Ibid.*, I, 174.

[27] See below, "The Beloved Community."

[28] I Corinthians 3:23, 15:28.

in history, and the process of salvation itself describes the course of history.[29]

Royce proposed to deal with three fundamental ideas[30] to be found in the thought of Paul, as a result of his attempt to explicate Christ's teaching: the idea of the Beloved Community (church), the idea of the inescapable moral burden of the individual (original sin), and the idea of Atonement (appearance of the Christ as mediator).[31] These three, said Royce, may be approached through the much debated idea of the Kingdom of Heaven. He suggested this because on his view the idea of the Kingdom of Heaven stood, for the early Christians, in special need of the greatest elaboration (as indeed it has ever since) and, in the attempt to provide such explication, the New Testament community produced the idea of the Christian Church. There can be little doubt that Royce is correct in his view that if any aspect of Christianity has been seen only "through a glass darkly," the idea of the Kingdom certainly has. From the very beginning of the tradition the most difficult questions have been raised: Is the kingdom of this world or of some other? Is it political in character or not? Is it wholly a matter of inner spiritual life or has it a visible form which is social?[32] All these and other questions concerning the kingdom were raised from the beginning and it is not incorrect to say that the divisions within Christianity can be traced to the variety of possible answers, and what is perhaps more important, to the variety of views concerning what it is that will decide the question. For as Royce correctly pointed out, however the

[29] See Reinhold Niebuhr, *The Nature and Destiny of Man*, II, 101f., and especially pp. 213ff. Here Niebuhr speaks of redemption in the Christ as a redemption "in principle" which remains to be completed "in fact."

[30] It is well to bear in mind that the term "idea" can be used here only if the element of symbol and myth contained in these "ideas" is taken into account, as Royce did.

[31] These ideas will no doubt surprise those accustomed to think of Royce merely as a moral idealist philosopher.

[32] These questions concern the correct interpretation of the following passages: John 18:36; Matt. 13:24-30, 13:31-32, 13:36-43; Luke 17:20-21. This last is the much debated ἡ Βασιλεία τοῦ Θεοῦ εντὸς ὑμῶν εστιν.

questions be answered, answers will not be found simply in what Luther in an unguarded moment referred to as the "plain meaning" of the texts. The "mind" of Christ may indeed be contained in the signs—that is, the biblical writings— which have been left, but there is no reading of these signs without interpretation. In the case of the idea of the kingdom, the problems are: what is the correct interpretation and who is the interpreter? The second question Royce answered by referring to the spirit in the community,[33] for he believed, as has been said, that it is the community that was first aware of the meaning of Jesus' teaching and of his mission. The first question, that of the correct interpretation of the kingdom, was also treated by that community, according to Royce, and in the course of interpreting that idea it came to articulate the three doctrines mentioned above as forming the subject of this discussion: the church, original sin, and atonement.

A brief statement of the general import of these ideas will be helpful. The following short extracts are from Royce's lecture on the problem with which he proposed to deal:

A. *The Beloved Community*
There is a certain universal and divine spiritual community. Membership in that community is necessary to the salvation of man.[34]

B. *The Moral Burden of the Individual*
The individual human being is by nature subject to some overwhelming moral burden from which, if unaided, he cannot escape.[35]

C. *Atonement*
The only escape for the individual, the only union with the divine spiritual community which he can obtain, is provided by the divine plan for the redemption of mankind. And this plan is one which includes an Atonement for the sins and for the guilt of mankind.[36]

The connection between these themes, on Royce's view, is that

[33] The Beloved Community, it will be remembered, is not *identical* with any historical institution.

[34] *The Problem of Christianity*, I, 39. It must never be forgotten that this community is not to be confused with any historical institution.

[35] *Ibid.*, I, 41. The burden of which Royce spoke includes both "sins" and "original sin."

[36] *Ibid.*, I, 43.

only atonement makes salvation possible, precisely because atonement makes possible the Beloved Community and, as will be shown, the necessary condition for salvation is to become a member of this community. These relations emerged from the experiences of the earliest Christian communities, in their attempt to offer a full and satisfying interpretation of the kingdom idea.

That Royce should have considered the community to be central is certainly consistent with his own outlook, and is also defensible independently on historical grounds. Not only does the tradition show that Jesus' own teaching was centered about that idea, but it is clear that a developing Christianity came to look upon a future universal community of believers as the concrete realization of that kingdom so vividly proclaimed by Jesus. In Royce's view of the matter, when the Christian community came to interpret the kingdom idea, to specify in detail the relation of each individual to God in the light of the life and death of the Christ, there emerged the three ideas mentioned above as essential to Christianity. These ideas may be said to express the Christian drama of salvation as follows: the individual person actually stands under the weight of a burden of guilt from which he cannot escape; salvation is offered in Christianity through the atoning work of the mediator who institutes, by his life and death, the community whose distinctive characteristic it is to be the redeeming community. The aim of Royce is to show by means of a philosophical analysis drawing upon all available evidence that the saving power of the community can be made intelligible and can be justified[37] by reference to both reason and the deepest human experience.

The fulfilment of such an aim requires a discussion of the Beloved Community in relation to the ideas of Sin and Atonement. This is done in the succeeding chapter.

[37] The sense in which any metaphysic or interpretation of existence can be said to be *justified* raises a problem going beyond the scope of this discussion. Certainly an interpretation of life and the world is not justified in the sense in which propositions in mechanics are verified, but it is possible, on the basis of continuing experience, to distinguish inadequate and fragmentary interpretations from others more inclusive, consistent and adequate to man's experience.

CHAPTER FIVE

THE BELOVED COMMUNITY

Having already briefly surveyed the development in Royce's view of the Absolute, as well as having indicated the theoretical, that is, the epistemological and metaphysical aspect of the theory of interpretation, it is necessary to turn now to the practical, that is, the ethical and religious, side of Royce's view that the true infinite is actual as a community of interpretation. The ethical and religious features of experience were interpreted most fully by Royce in the theory of what he called the beloved community, and it is this theory which must now be examined. Such an examination, however, must not lose sight of the fact that, while Royce's conception of the infinite as a community of interpretation is, on its theoretical side, a solution of the old problem of the actual infinite, the ethical and religious features of his community theory are definitely to be taken as a solution to the later "problem of Christianity" outlined in the previous chapter. This is not to say that there is no connection between his position here and his earlier analyses of religious and ethical problems. On the contrary, his earlier views, particularly in *The Philosophy of Loyalty* and *The Sources of Religious Insight*, are in accord with the theory of the beloved community. What must not be overlooked, however, is that Royce's whole argument in *The Problem of Christianity* must be understood in the light of what he considered the "problem of Christianity" to be. For the theory of community is his proposed solution to that problem.

Before proceeding, one further introductory word is necessary, and it concerns the method to be followed. Since Royce's analysis of such ideas as sin and atonement are necessarily connected with his theory of the beloved community, or the church, it is important that these ideas be considered in their relations to one another as Royce considered them in his own discussion.

The Beloved Community

There can be little question that the idea of the church in the Christian tradition, whether it be Augustine's, Aquinas' or Luther's, is an instance of the making explicit of an idea which, although it may be shown to be *contained in*[1] certain teachings of Jesus, certainly is not at all clearly and positively stated in his teaching.[2] Therefore, Royce was correct in pointing out that, although Jesus' traditional teaching centers about the idea of the kingdom of God or of heaven,[3] it was only after the death of Jesus that the attempt to develop the kingdom idea in concrete terms led to a thoroughgoing doctrine of the church.

Before pushing the analysis further it is necessary to call attention to one highly significant point. By the terms "church" or "beloved community" Royce never meant to denote an historical institution like the Roman church, the Eastern Orthodox church, or the Presbyterian church. He referred to what has been called the "invisible church" in the Christian tradition, and this company of the redeemed is, as Protestantism has correctly affirmed, known in its fulness only to God. Hence it does not coincide with any finite and historical establishment however infallible it may claim to be.[4] Royce, on the other hand, was well aware of the need for some concrete embodiment of community

---

[1] "Contained in" here cannot mean "part of what is asserted" as, for example, "there are more than seven people in this room" is part of what is asserted by "there are ten people in this room." In the case of the sayings of Jesus, "contained in" must be taken to mean "capable of being interpreted as," that is, there are sayings attributed to Jesus which are capable of being interpreted as referring to a church.

[2] Of course Matt. 16:18 will be cited as contradicting this, but any New Testament scholar knows the enormous difficulties surrounding this verse. Scholars not already committed to the Roman or Anglo-Catholic point of view generally regard it as an addition to the text in the interest of the developing church, or interpret it as a play on the words Πέτρος, πέτρα.

[3] There is some question about the equivalence of the terms "God" and "heaven." They are used synonymously in the *Mishna*. See A. Robertson, *Regnum Dei*, pp. 62f.

[4] See *The Sources of Religious Insight*, pp. 272ff., for a more complete statement of this point.

for the achievement of specific tasks and for this reason he thought
of the various empirical churches as being in a position to bring
about the community which is as wide as mankind itself, despite
the fact that no one of these churches can pretend to be more than
a part of the larger unity which God seeks to establish through
them. In order for the visible churches to play their part effectively they must, according to Royce, have a clear vision of the
beloved community in its ideal completion, and such a vision as
they do possess must not be obscured by narrowness of insight
or self-righteousness.[5]

The relation between the church visible and the church invisible is not one upon which it is necessary to dwell at length here.
It is important to be clear about Royce's use of the term, however.

To return to the main point, the origin of the doctrine of
the church, while it is not possible in this discussion to enter
fully into current views of the matter—it can be said that there
is considerable agreement among scholars on one point at least:
that the New Testament community came to regard itself, the
church, as the New Jerusalem made possible by the life and work
of the Christ. This new community, the ἐκκλησία of Christ, that
is, the company of those devoted to Him, supersedes the Old
Testament conception of the kingdom of God as the "kingdom
of our Father David."[6] In Paul's teaching, the kingdom or
ἐκκλησία of Christ is distinguished from the kingdom of God
in that the former is a present reality for believers, while the
latter remains as the symbol of God's ultimate reconciliation

[5] It is very interesting to note one shift in Royce's position on this head. In
The Sources of Religious Insight, p. 280, the true church is said to be obscured by
our *ignorance* and *narrowness of insight*. This suggests that the obstacles are such as
might be overcome by knowledge alone. In *The Problem of Christianity*, Royce held
what some present-day thinkers would call a "realistic" view. He said, "Least
of all may we attempt, as many do, to accuse this or that special tendency or
power in the actual Church, past or present, of being mainly responsible for this
failure to appreciate the ideal church. The defect lies deeper than students of such
problems usually suppose. Human nature,—not any one party,—yes, the very
nature of the processes of growth themselves and not any particular form of
religious or of moral errors, must be viewed as the source of the principal tragedies
of the history of all the Christian ideals" (I, 57f.).

[6] Mark 11:10.

with the world, the bringing of the kingdom of Christ to completion, or in Paul's language, the situation in which God is "all in all."[7] This latter distinction would correspond to Royce's distinction between the beloved community as it is partially realized at a given moment in history and the final completion of that community as the universal kingdom of God.

Nevertheless Royce seems unaware of the distinction between the kingdom of God and that of Christ, although it is in the New Testament in Paul's thought and it was also emphasized by Calvin.[8] This latter might be taken as evidence against regarding Royce as a Calvinist, yet Royce's failure to use Calvin's language should not obscure the fact that the distinction is implied in all that Royce had to say concerning the church. He thought of the church, taken as the community of the faithful on earth, as the instrument through which God's ultimate purpose is to be accomplished, and this is precisely Calvin's position. The following paragraph from Royce makes this quite clear:

When the Christian Church began, in the Apostolic Age, to take visible form, the idea of the mission of the Church expressed the meaning which the Christian community came to attach to the social implications of the founder's doctrine. What was merely hinted in the parables now became explicit. The Kingdom of Heaven was to be realized in and through and for the Church,—in the fellowship of the faithful who constituted the Church as it was on earth; through the divine Spirit that was believed to guide the life of the Church; and for the future experience of the Church whenever the end should come, and whenever the purpose of God should finally be manifested and accomplished.[9]

Howsoever the doctrine of the church may finally be formulated by Christianity, the point germane to this study is that the doctrine represents an explicit interpretation of earlier sayings which were developed in the efforts of the growing Christian community to understand the teachings of Jesus in regard to the kingdom of God. That Jesus spoke in parables is a well-known fact, as is also the fact that some of the most familiar of these

[7] I Cor. 15:28. See A. Robertson, *Regnum Dei*, pp. 48ff.
[8] See, for example, *The Institutes of the Christian Religion*, Bk. IV, Ch. I, Sec. V.
[9] *The Problem of Christianity*, I, 50f.

have to do with the kingdom. It is because Jesus employed this medium of communication that an interpretation is called for at every point, and every proposed interpretation must inevitably pass beyond what the parables themselves assert. It was of vital importance to the early community, as Royce correctly pointed out, to interpret the parables of the kingdom correctly and, at the same time, to define the function of the actual community, the fellowship of the faithful on earth, in the realization of the final kingdom in which God's purpose would be achieved.

Royce thus regarded the interpretation of the kingdom idea made by the early Christian community as an addition to the original[10] doctrine, but an addition which is not (and historically was not) to be taken as less important on that account. Royce believed that for the primitive community some view about the function of the church was an essential mark of the Christian believer, and one which came to be at least as important as any specific teaching of Jesus preserved by the tradition. It must of course be admitted that too much stress can be placed upon this fact, and certain "ecclesiastical" strains within Christianity have done so. On the other hand, those who have put a doctrine of the church at the center of Christianity have historically meant by the church a particular institution marked by officials or clergy, and this is what Royce did *not* mean. For Royce (and he is definitely on Paul's side here), the church always means the community in the spirit which, though it must be embodied—that is, be "visible"—is never to be *identified with* any of its outward forms. Further, as will become clear, Royce was concerned with the church only in so far as it is the sphere or "region of" (to use Moberly's expression) of the divine love which alone has the power to redeem the individual. Since the problem of Christianity finally turns upon the possibility of the modern individual's affirmation that the beloved community in its saving power is real, Royce was concerned with the beloved community as redemptive community. Hence he confined himself to consideration of this aspect of the church, to the neglect of all others.

[10] "Original" here means "the traditional expressions of Jesus himself on the kingdom in so far as these can be recovered by scientific research."

In order to carry out his enterprise of interpreting the essential Christian ideas, Royce turned first to certain considerations drawn from anthropology and social psychology which are relevant to an analysis of universal community, because he wanted ultimately to show the basis in actual experience which the Christian idea of the beloved community has. In *The Problem of Christianity*, Royce followed his earlier analysis of the community to be found mainly in *The Philosophy of Loyalty*.[11] In the later work he restated his thesis that the community is not simply a collection of individuals, but rather a unity which endures; that social products, such as language, arts, customs, etc., bespeak a mind for the community which is identical neither with a particular individual member nor with the collection; and that, under certain conditions, communities tend to be organized into more inclusive communities embracing greater numbers of members. All these features of community which were emphasized earlier by Royce were repeated by him in order to serve as a basis for the analysis of the beloved community.

In reply to the possible objection that to speak of the community in such terms is to speak (a) mystically or (b) metaphorically, Royce called attention to the work of Wilhelm Wundt, the German social psychologist. Royce pointed out that, in his *Völkerpsychologie*, Wundt adopted the idea of a *Gesamtbewusstsein* (collective consciousness) on purely psychological grounds. Royce held that Wundt's concept is not mystical in character, nor can it be regarded as a mere metaphor, precisely because it was suggested by Wundt's own empirical investigations and it enabled him to connect certain data not otherwise explicable. Royce called Wundt's procedure a "pragmatic" one, because he recognized the fact that for him the ascription of a mind to the community was a "working hypothesis."[12]

Royce's primary concern was the ethical and religious implications of such an understanding of the nature of community.

[11] *The Sources of Religious Insight* also contains valuable material on his idea of the nature and function of the community.

[12] See *The Problem of Christianity*, I, 64f. The materials for a fuller study of Royce's debt to Wundt are wanting.

An individual, said Royce, not only may, but often does regard the social unities to which he belongs, family, village, town, nation, etc., as beings of a super-personal sort.[13] And the individual may find in a complete devotion to that super-personal unity the answer to the question of his own destiny and fulfilment. It is such devotion that Royce called *loyalty*, and although loyalty seems to be inseparably connected with religion for Royce, he continually emphasized the wealth and variety of concrete enterprises in which the spirit of loyalty plays an all-important part. These concrete enterprises may be as different as the carrying on of scientific investigation or the campaigning for the election of some candidate for office, but the same thoroughgoing devotion (loyalty) on the part of the individuals involved to the cause which is above them all remains. It is this super-personal reality, or the cause, which is at the foundation of the community.[14]

Royce, as is so clear in the earlier *Philosophy of Loyalty*, looked upon the loyal spirit as the means whereby the isolated individual is brought into the presence of that cause devotion to which constitutes his moral fulfilment or, in the case of the beloved community, his "salvation."[15] Historically, Royce contended, the community has always played the role of providing men with a supreme value devotion to which results in individual self-realization and a super-personal unity of many in one at the same time. He cited the Stoic faith in universal community as an illustration of the spirit of loyalty in a purely human form extending to embrace all mankind. He wished to call attention to the part played by loyalty in human history, apart from historic religion, for he was anxious to show that community has had an important function in human experience and one not necessarily connected with religion. In other words, Royce was trying to analyze various other features of community in all its forms before

---

[13] See Herbert W. Schneider, *A History of American Philosophy*, pp. 489, 490.

[14] *The Problem of Christianity*, I, 68; also *The Philosophy of Loyalty*, pp. 16f.

[15] Royce's language often conveys the impression that it is "individuality" from which men must be saved. Such is not the case. *Individualism*, containing an element of spiritual self-assertion and pride, is what is the evil for Royce, and salvation for him consists in becoming a member of the community which trains true individuals and at the same time overcomes the sins of *individualism*.

considering the beloved community whose proper aim is redemption.

The most striking feature of Royce's discussion of the Christian community is his view of the relation of Jesus to that community. From the outset he made it clear that the controversy between Fundamentalism and Modernism concerning the status of Jesus is a fruitless one because much that is of central importance is overlooked in the traditional formulation of the issue. As usually debated, the issue is: Is Jesus "really divine" or is he to be regarded as a "mere human"? and, it must be borne in mind, it is generally assumed that these alternatives are both exhaustive and incompatible.[16] Royce expressed his dissatisfaction with both Fundamentalism and Modernism on the question of Jesus' nature. Modernism[17] is wrong, because it seeks to reduce Jesus to the perfect individual and because it completely ignores the redemptive power of the body of Christ, which was so much emphasized by Paul. On the other hand, he likewise rejected the naive supernaturalism of orthodoxy, because of its literal dependence on dubious legends and witnesses as well as its appeal to authority, all to the neglect of concrete human experience. Consequently, Royce had little to say about the "person" of Christ as the problem has been traditionally set, but he had a great deal to say about the nature and work of Jesus in relation to the community and this "bears upon the very core of the Gospel."[18]

Royce took as his point of departure the contrast between what the biblical tradition reports of Jesus' teaching about the kingdom and salvation and the views of Paul on the meaning of atonement and redemption in relation to the body of Christ or the church. By focussing attention on the redemptive power which the Christian community came to ascribe to Christ, Royce hoped to make clearer what traditionally has been meant by the "person" of Christ. Some form of love, said Royce, is what Jesus both embodied and preached, and this is what redeems, according to Christianity. He therefore suggested that to under-

[16] The inadequacy of this approach is further suggested by the fact that the tradition has always sought to maintain that in some sense *both* affirmations are true.

[17] Royce was largely dependent on Harnack for his view of "Modernism."

[18] *Ibid.*, I, 75.

stand the essence of Christianity as a religion of redemption one must first understand the redeeming power of that form of love which is divine. Penetration to the depth of this problem leads right back to the "person" of the founder of Christianity, precisely because it is the essence of the Christ to be the redeemer, as the New Testament community well knew, and apart from this function the Christ has no "person." This is why, on Royce's view, when we discover what it is that is redemptive in Christianity, we will discover at the same time both the nature and function of the Christ. It is on the basis of such profound considerations as these that Royce felt justified in neglecting further discussion of the humanity or the divinity of Christ in favor of an analysis of that love which is redemptive.

Royce's analysis is by no means exhaustive in detail, nor is it possible here to follow him even as far as he went, but it must be borne in mind that Royce was well-acquainted with the results of modern scholarship which bear on the Judeo-Christian tradition, and hence whatever shortcomings his interpretation may contain should not be too simply attributed to the limitations of a philosophical approach which is supposed not to be in touch with the facts. Royce commenced by pointing out that for Jesus "the duty of man, the essence of religion, and the Kingdom of Heaven itself"[19] are all described in terms of the ideal of love so vividly set forth in such parables as the prodigal son, the lost sheep and the laborers in the vineyard. And Royce was aware, as students of the New Testament have ever been, that this norm of love in Jesus' teaching is stated only in the most general terms, and consequently that the follower of Jesus is faced with a perplexing problem—that of mediating between the absolute law of love ($\dot{\alpha}\gamma\dot{\alpha}\pi\eta$) and the endless variety of contingent situations which make up the life of both men and nations. Royce recognized this problem and frankly acknowledged, as most great Christian thinkers have done,[20] that Jesus'

[19] *Ibid.*, I, 76.

[20] See, for example, Reinhold Niebuhr, *An Interpretation of Christian Ethics*, p. 39. Cf. *The Problem of Christianity*, I, 86.

teaching leaves the whole multiplicity of practical problems unsolved. It is at this point, said Royce, that the experience of the later Christian community becomes highly significant. The interpretations to be found in the letters of Paul which arose from his experience within the Christian communities represent an expansion of Jesus' teaching, to be sure, but an expansion designed to meet just those concrete problems with which the ethic of Jesus, as found in his sayings, does not deal. Royce maintained that these contributions of Paul to a concrete understanding of Christian love must not be regarded as additions having only secondary importance,[21] but that they must be valued highly because Paul conceived them as due to the guidance of that spirit which, as the early community believed, led unto all truth,[22] and because "Paul's additional thought," to use Royce's language, "was a critical influence in determining both the evolution and the permanent meaning of Christianity."[23]

After having sought to justify the significance of Pauline thought on the subject of redeeming love, Royce proceeded to a more direct analysis of the Christian idea of love. At the outset he wisely rejected the identification of the Christian norm with what has often been called self-effacement or "pure altruism," the favorite expression of the nineteenth-century moral and political philosophers.[24] In Royce's opinion such an identification is an error because, besides other reasons, the love of God and of neighbor commanded by Jesus necessarily involves a reference to the infinite value of the individual person as the object of God's love. Therefore the essence of the love which the Christian is commanded to manifest cannot require the self-destruction of the individual self. Furthermore, as Christianity

[21] See Reinhold Niebuhr, *Christianity and Power Politics*, *passim*, on the problem of the so-called "Pauline accretions."

[22] John 16:13.

[23] *The Problem of Christianity*, I, 78.

[24] Royce would also have rejected Mill's attempt to identify the ethic of Jesus with the principle of utility. See *Utilitarianism*, ed. "Little Library of Liberal Arts," p. 18.

has always held, it is only through individual selves that the redeeming love of God can be manifested. Royce was correct in calling attention to the error of equating Christian love with altruism, but the main reason why it is an error is simpler than he suggests. The love of God and neighbor is one in which the self as lover cannot be negated, because we are commanded to love God and neighbor "as thy self," in the words of the biblical text. Christianity, as Kierkegaard expressed it so well, presupposes "that a man loves himself"[25] and then commands love to the neighbor by the same man in exactly the same measure. In so far as this faithfully follows the intention of Jesus, it is correct to say that one can have no idea of the measure of the love which the Christian is to manifest, apart from the love of self.[26]

The meaning of love of God and of the neighbor must now be clarified. Love of God, said Royce, may be clearly defined in religious[27] terms as purity of heart, perfect sincerity and complete devotion. It is clear that the person who embodies these virtues illustrates what is meant by love of God, but concerning the meaning of love of neighbor difficulties arise which are by no means easily overcome. It is far from clear, said Royce, how the Christian is to manifest the spirit of love in all the multifarious situations involving many men in a highly technical society. As far as the general prescription of extending love to all men in order to bring them into community is concerned, there is no problem. This commandment is clear, but when confronted with a particular "neighbor" in a specific situation, the problem arises as to what concrete acts do in fact manifest love toward that person. Such a problem cannot be solved simply by appealing to the teachings which the tradition attributes to Jesus. Royce saw this; hence he said, "Jesus has no system of rules to expound

[25] *Works of Love*, p. 16. See also I, Ch. II, A, *passim*, on this head.

[26] Augustine has a clear and vivid discussion of this point. See *De Doctr. Christ.* Bk. I, Chs. XXIII, XXVI.

[27] Implicit in Royce's analysis is the distinction between the religious and the ethical domains; love of God (religion) and love of neighbor (ethics). See F. H. Bradley, *Ethical Studies* (1927 ed.), pp. 313ff. for what is perhaps the clearest philosophical statement of the relations between these two domains.

for guiding the single acts of the philanthropic life."[28] He also recognized that Jesus (and this is evident to any reader of the gospels) depended for the Christian life upon individual instinct informed by love rather than upon any set of rules for guiding conduct such as is to be found, for instance, in Jewish legal writing.[29]

What is of particular importance at this juncture is Royce's clear insight into the nature of the difficulty surrounding the meaning of love of neighbor. The other self, said Royce, the neighbor, is always to a greater or lesser degree a "mystery" to all the other selves who come in contact with him. According to his view, the fact that a given individual is never in a position to comprehend any other individual fully or to know his final destiny, makes it impossible for any one self to know exactly what an expression of Christian love to that other self in a given case would be. This is a highly significant insight, and one often overlooked in discussions of these matters, for it provides a clear reply to the frequent objection of many modern minds to the ethic of Jesus because it presumably does not tell you "what to do" in every conceivable situation. Such an objection is justified on the surface because Jesus did not and could not anticipate every possible state of affairs in which men find themselves, but the deeper explanation is that men themselves are "mysterious" in the sense that no self is ever in a position to know enough about the nature and destiny of another self to be absolutely sure what course of action would be consistent with the love towards that self that is commanded.[30] This is why it is ultimately God and God alone who must fulfill each personality through his love because God alone possesses the truth about each personality. Royce correctly pointed out that Jesus takes this very view of the situation himself and he therefore trusts God's love implicitly

[28] *The Problem of Christianity*, I, 86.

[29] The difference here is between what Bradley would call choosing on the basis of what is *in* the mind and on the basis of rules *before* the mind.

[30] See *The Religious Aspect of Philosophy*, pp. 468ff. for a discussion of this same problem. At that time Royce sought a solution in terms not of the community (see below), but of the Absolute thought and infinite judge who knows and judges all as one.

and looks to the coming end of the world when love in its perfection will triumph in the establishment of the divine kingdom.

Yet the question must naturally arise at this point: How shall each one treat his neighbor in the "meantime?"[31] Obviously the end is not yet nor is the kingdom fulfilled, and God, to be sure, alone possesses the truth about the individual, but yet as actual persons attempting to live the Christian life we still stand under the necessity of obeying the commands. Royce tried to show that the experience of Paul provides the Christian answer to this question, and to this end he proceeded by raising the further question: "What does Paul contribute to this doctrine of love?"[32] Paul's contribution cannot be understood apart from a new element in his experience which is of central importance. This new element, said Royce, is a new being, the body of Christ, the divine community of which Christ is the head. It is with this community that a new beginning, so to speak, is made by Christianity, which has a direct bearing on Paul's interpretation of Christian love. Royce viewed Paul as one who considered himself possessed of a further revelation of the spirit in the idea and concrete reality of the church or the beloved community. That Paul does indeed refer to the community of the faithful as the body of Christ and also that he thinks of it as having a super-personal reality are facts well known to students of Pauline thought, and in this respect Royce's analysis is consonant with the facts.[33] The significance of the community for the problem of love lies in the function which it has in overcoming the chasms between individuals and in eliminating to a degree the mysterious character of the individual personality. Royce said, "For Paul the neighbor

[31] The "meantime" is what New Testament scholars have referred to as the "interim period" and many interpret the ethic of Jesus solely as an interim ethic, that is, as an ethic relevant only on the assumption that the concrete world between Jesus' coming and the final judgment, the "meantime," would soon pass and the kingdom be established. Extended discussion is beyond this study.

[32] *The Problem of Christianity*, I, 91.

[33] Some of the relevant New Testament passages are as follows: I Cor. 12: 12–27; Col. 1:16–18, 24–29; Eph. 2:19–22. The Pauline authorship of Ephesians has been questioned by some, however. See E. F. Scott, *The Literature of the New Testament*, p. 180.

has now become a being who is primarily the fellow member of the Christian community."[34] The neighbor as a member of the same community to which one also belongs begins to be less mysterious because a common loyalty involving a common memory (ideal past) and a common hope (ideal future) is shared by both, and when the question, What shall I do for my neighbor? is raised, the common elements introduced by the community make the answer less problematic. For Royce this meant that Christian love is inseparably bound to the community precisely because the neighbor is both defined and known as a fellow member of it.

The special transformation of Christian love made by Paul, according to Royce, is that he interprets love as *loyalty*. Salvation can now be defined in terms of the relation between the individual and the beloved community. The goal of life can be found only through loyalty to that community which embraces all the "neighbors" and is at the same time the object of God's love and concern. Paul, said Royce, saw in the ideal of the divine community the fulfilment of both the prophetic view of the ultimate triumph of God in his kingdom and of the teaching of Jesus concerning the love of individuals one for the other. Concerning Paul's outlook on both these themes, Royce said:

> If the Corinthians unlovingly contend, brother with brother, concerning their gifts, Paul tells them about the body of Christ, and about the divine unity of its spirit in all the diversity of its members and of their powers. On the other hand, if it is loyalty to the Church which is to be interpreted and revivified, Paul pictures the dignity of the spiritual community in terms of the direct beauty and sweetness and tenderness of the love of brother for brother—that love which seeketh not her own.[35]

Perhaps Royce's analysis would have been clearer if he had made more direct use of his own distinction between religion and ethics. Religion for him has to do with the ultimate meaning of life and the final destiny of the individual as related to God, while ethics concerns the relations between persons in society.

[34] *The Problem of Christianity*, I, 97.
[35] *Ibid.*, I, 101.

This division is clearly expressed in the central Christian commandment, love of God (religion) and love of neighbor (ethics). What Royce meant by loyalty to the community, or the body of Christ, represents the religious dimension, for there the individual loves God through complete devotion to the beloved community. What he meant by individuals manifesting that love which preserves the unity of the Christian body and at the same time fosters right relations between persons represents the ethical dimension. Love in both its forms centers about the community whose very structure foreshadows the kingdom of heaven.

Royce found the central importance of Paul's contribution to the development of Christianity in his interpretation of Christianity as a religion of loyalty; the primary loyalty of the Christian as one who loves God is to Christ, present as the mystical body, or church, and the primary loyalty of the Christian as one who loves his neighbor is care for that neighbor as a member of the beloved community. The secret of Paul's power among the early Christians, according to Royce, was the manner in which he kept both of these objects of devotion clearly before his own mind and the minds of his followers. Loyalty to that community established by the Christ provides the individual Christian with a concrete expression of his love towards God, and that very same community makes it possible for the individual to love his neighbor by enabling him to discover what deeds would really express love towards that neighbor. It is this latter feature which is Paul's significant expansion of Jesus' teaching.

The community makes possible such intimate relations between its members that each one is better able to bridge the gap between his own self and every other. The individual selves, according to Royce, thereby become less mysterious and the question: What shall I do for my brother? becomes easier to answer precisely because the brother is a member of the same community to which one also belongs. The community brings its members close together by uniting them in a common memory and a common hope.

Royce concluded his discussion of the beloved community by calling attention to Paul's view of the church as the concrete embodiment of that ideal kingdom both envisaged by the Old Testament prophets and spoken of by Jesus. Of this beloved community he said, in summary:

This, the first of our three essential ideas of Christianity, is the idea of a spiritual life in which universal love for all individuals shall be completely blended, practically harmonized, with an absolute loyalty for a real and universal community. God, the neighbor, and the one Church: These three are for Paul the objects of Christian love and the inspiration of the life of love.[36]

The Moral Burden of the Individual

This second of the three essential Christian ideas to which Royce directed attention will no doubt cause some surprise to those accustomed to thinking of him only as an idealist and an optimist. To know that Royce has a studied and sharply defined idea of sin is very important for an understanding of his interpretation of Christianity. This, more than anything else in his thought, marks him off from much that has gone by the name of "liberal theology" in America. L. P. Jacks expressed this very well when he said of Royce, "Nothing could be further from his way than the undiscriminating optimism into which Liberalism has so often degenerated."[37] In discussing the relation between religion and morality in *The Sources of Religious Insight*, Royce made it clear that concerning human nature he was no simple optimist. He said:

Suppose that we are in agreement in holding that there is a highest good.

Nevertheless the question: How far is man naturally in danger of missing this supreme good? is a question, which, since we are all fallible mortals, leaves room for many varieties of opinion . . . to me the religious need seems an insistent and clear need. But many moralists are partisans of duty as a substitute for religion. And they are often much more optimistic regarding human nature than I am.[38]

[36] *Ibid.*, I, 105.

[37] *Hibbert Journal*, XII (1913), p. 216.

[38] *The Sources of Religious Insight*, pp. 172f. By "religious need" Royce understood the need of man to be absolved from guilt and sin and thereby be regenerated.

Royce knew that *moralism* in all its forms conceives of man as a being possessing no defect which is not in principle capable of being overcome through moral striving, and that consequently for such an outlook talk about salvation in purely religious terms is either meaningless or fanatical. Royce, on the other hand, did find the idea of salvation in religious terms meaningful, because he was no optimist concerning human nature. He believed that man is in danger of failure in his attempt to reach his ideal, because of defects in his own nature, and that on this account man stands in need of the salvation of which Judaism, Buddhism and Christianity have variously conceived. It is with the nature of these defects ("moral burden" or "sin") that Royce was primarily concerned in his discussion of the second of the three essential ideas he has selected.

At the heart of Royce's idea of the nature of sin is his view of what may be called the dialectic between the individual and the social environment within which his development takes place. His central thesis, already foreshadowed in the discussion of individualism in *The Philosophy of Loyalty*, is that the rebellious and self-willed individual who sets himself up exclusively as his own end is the product of social training and of upbringing, and that consequently to look upon the salvation or redemption of individuals as achievable in purely natural social terms is an error. For, said Royce, our higher forms of social and cultural life left to themselves tend only to increase the difficulty precisely because they produce that very self-willed individual who stands in need of redemption. The similarity between this view, even as briefly sketched, and the view of both the Old Testament writers and of Paul on the subject is apparent. The prophetic criticism against the city (standing for "culture" and its pretensions as in the" tower of Babel" myth), and Paul's attack upon the sufficiency of worldly wisdom and resources, both direct attention to what Royce had in mind; the natural defects to which man is subject cannot be overcome through the "natural" cultivation of man's distinctive and higher powers (intelligence and foresight) because it is precisely this cultivation which increases the evil by producing that individual pride and self-assertiveness which is at the root of man's original sin and consequently brings about his alienation from God.

If we distinguish, said Royce, between our conduct and our consciousness of our conduct, this distinction leads directly to the problem of the source of that consciousness, or conscience.[39] As has already been pointed out, all self-consciousness requires the community because no self can know itself and judge its conduct without recourse to the processes of comparison and interpretation, and this involves reference to other selves and their deeds. Conscience, for Royce, can never arise apart from social training in so far as it involves comparison of the self with other selves and consequent interpretation of the nature and meaning of one's deeds. But the dual and even paradoxical aspect of the process according to which conscience develops consists in the fact that such social training brings about a considerable discrepancy between individual conduct and the individual's judgment upon his conduct. Outwardly, according to Royce, the individual may conform to the social will as a result of training,[40] but since it is through this very process of social intercourse with its conflicts and tensions that individual self-consciousness arises, the person will be trained in self-assertiveness at the same time simply because his own heightened awareness of himself leads him to regard himself as a final and exclusive end. The following section from Royce's analysis states this development very well:

If the individual is not defective or degenerate, but a fairly good member of his stock, his conduct may be trained by effective social discipline into a more or less admirable conformity to the standards of the general will. But his conduct is not the same as his own consciousness about his conduct; or, in other words, his deeds and his ideals are not necessarily in mutual agreement. Meanwhile his consciousness about his conduct, his ideals, his conscience, are all trained, under ordinary conditions, by a social process that begins in tensions, in rivalries, in contests,

[39] Royce consistently used the term "conscience" to refer to "consciousness about our conduct and some judgment on it."

[40] See *The Problem of Christianity*, I, 177, where Royce spoke of social training as leading to *respect* for the law, but not to *love* for it.

and that naturally continues, the farther it goes, to become more and more a process which introduces new and more complex conflicts.

This evil constantly increases. The burden grows heavier. Society can, by its ordinary skill, train many to be its servants—servants who, being under rigid discipline, submit because they must. But precisely in proportion as society becomes more skillful in the external forms of culture, it trains its servants by a process that breeds spiritual enemies. That is, it breeds men who, even when they keep the peace, are inwardly enemies one of another; because every man, in a highly cultivated social world, is trained to moral self-consciousness by his social conflicts. And these same men are inwardly enemies of the collective social will itself, because in a highly cultivated social order the social will is oppressively vast, and the individual is trained to self-consciousness by a process which shows him the contrast between his own will and this, which so far seems to him a vast impersonal social will. He may obey. That is conduct. But he will naturally revolt inwardly; and that is his inevitable form of spiritual self-assertion. . . .[41]

Royce considered this process as one in which the individual is involved necessarily,[42] and he looked upon the development as having unfortunate consequences which the individual must continue to bear. Social cultivation, said Royce, may be viewed as training "under the law," to use Pauline language, but the paradox of this training consists in the fact that individual*ism* and its consequent rebellion against the law are the final outcome. This is a distinctive feature of Royce's thought and one which throws some light on his interpretation of salvation through the community. Royce did not look upon men as merely isolated individuals who are to be "saved" by joining a community. His is no simple doctrine of "social salvation." Rather Royce held that the human situation is one in which increasing social cultivation aggravates the evil because it results in individual*ism*, and individualism, far from being the starting point, is the late product of civilization. He said:

As we all know, individualism, viewed as a highly potent social tendency, is a product of high cultivation. It is also a relatively modern

[41] *Ibid.*, I, 142f.

[42] See *ibid.*, I, 151. "Now this my divided state, this my distraction of will, is no mishap of my private fortune. It belongs to the human race, as a race capable of high moral cultivation." Cf. p. 155.

product of such cultivation. Savages appear to know little about individualism.[43]

In the light of these considerations salvation, if it is to be at all meaningful for the individual, must not consist simply in making a transition from an individual to a social level, but in the establishment of that special community which does not breed individualism because it embodies some higher and therefore super-human form of love powerful enough to transform the individual and at the same time do away with the fatal outcome of natural social cultivation which is based on nothing higher than human talents and potentialities.

In his attempt to interpret the Christian view of man's moral burden, Royce first sought to understand the attitude of the "modern man" towards the ancient problem of sin.[44] To this end he had recourse to the essay by Matthew Arnold on "St. Paul and Protestantism," because he believed that what Arnold echoed in that essay is fairly typical of what the enlightened mind of his time would have had to say on the subject. Royce, of course, had nothing to do with judging either Arnold's criticism of Protestantism or his view of Paul and Jesus. His sole concern was with this essay as a characteristically modern view of the problem of sin. The ideas singled out for special emphasis by Royce are: Arnold's stricture against excessive brooding over sin (a brooding which Arnold took to be a characteristic peculiar to Puritanism), and his consequent counsel to "get rid of sin." The means to the achievement of this end, according to Arnold, is to be found in the experience of Paul, who "died to sin" because he "fell in love with" the spirit of the man Jesus. This, Royce commented, represents a view of the matter which the modern mind, if it is not altogether indifferent to such problems, finds congenial, and it is in the light of this view that he set out to consider the classic Christian conception in more detail.

In attempting to define sin as it is found in the sayings of

[43] *Ibid.*, I, 145.

[44] By "original sin," Royce meant the individual self-assertion characteristic of the process of development he had outlined. By "conscious sin," he meant deliberate acts of disloyalty to the community (see below).

Jesus, Royce rightly recognized that if, for Jesus, the measure of the deed is always the *inwardness* of the doer, the whole-heartedness of one's love for God as the basis of the deed, as he put it, then sin must consist in either the absence of such a love, or in some direct defiance of it. As such, sin means separation from God, or, as Royce expressed it, "alienation from the Kingdom and from the Father."[45] He noted that the alienation which is sin and the ultimate destruction which is its consequence are both to be found in Jesus' teaching, and hence that these ideas cannot simply be set aside, as later so-called theological "accretions." Yet, as Royce was aware, thè destruction of the sinner is not the last word which Christianity has to offer. Christian faith envisages a way out for man, a way involving repentance. Repentance, however, is possible for the sinner only if he receives some assistance from beyond himself. In the course of time the developing Christian community came to regard such necessary assistance as *in some sense*[46] the work of Christ. Royce said, referring to the fundamental Christian conviction *that* Christ saved from sin, although *how* might still remain a mystery:

> A corollary of this central teaching was a further opinion which tradition also emphasized, and, for centuries emphasized the more, the further the apostolic age receded into the past. This further opinion was: That the wilful sinner is powerless to return to a wholehearted union with God through any deed of his own. He could not "get rid of sin," either by means of repentance or otherwise, unless the work of Christ had prepared the way.[47]

In addition to this there is one further feature of the Christian understanding of sin to which Royce called attention, and that is the idea that unforgiven sin leads to the "death" of the sinner. Royce pointed out that, while the Hebrew prophets had already spoken of both a penalty for a life of unrighteousness and of the "death" of the unrepentant one whom Jahweh could cast off, the Christian community came to link the idea of a penalty

[45] *Ibid.*, I, 229.

[46] The history of the idea of atonement represents the various attempts which have been made to say exactly in what sense this is true.

[47] *Ibid.*, I, 231f.

for unforgiven sin with certain beliefs about eternal life which were only dimly understood in the history of Hebrew religion. Hence the idea of the "second death" arose, and Christian thinkers began to interpret, by means of symbol and myth, the "death" which the unforgiven sinner merits as an endless penalty from which there is no escape. On the basis of the foregoing considerations, Royce summed up the Christian doctrine of the wilful sin of the individual in two theses:

1. By no deed of his own, unaided by the supernatural consequences of the work of Christ, can the wilful sinner win forgiveness.
2. The penalty of unforgiven sin is the endless second death.[48]

Having indicated briefly both the classic Christian view of sin and the view of the "modern man," who, as Royce put it, "does not believe in hell, and who is too busy to think about his own sins,"[49] he directed his attention to the task of interpreting[50] the contrast that has resulted. Royce believed that the ideas of sin and of sin's inevitable punishment are not understood by the modern mind mainly because of the stress which the enlightened mind has come to put on the dignity and autonomy of man as an essentially moral being.[51] It is this emphasis that leads the modern mind to reject as unjust the idea of an endless punishment seemingly arbitrarily imposed by some divine power. "The just penalty of sin, to the modern mind," said Royce, "must therefore be the penalty, whatever it is, which the enlightened sinner, if fully awake to the nature of his deed . . . would voluntarily inflict upon himself."[52] In view of this, the modern man finds little if any meaning in the notion of an endless penalty for sin.

Royce admitted that there is a real difficulty here which is not to be passed over lightly, and one which requires for its

[48] Ibid., I, 235.
[49] Ibid., I, 236.
[50] It should be clear that Royce's method in these lectures is an illustration of the same process of interpretation he has analyzed so well.
[51] This does not refer to man's goodness but simply to his capacity for reflecting on his conduct and appraising it.
[52] Ibid., I, 237.

elimination a process of careful and sympathetic interpretation. He rejected at the outset, however, the attempt made by liberal Christianity to reconcile the modern mind with itself by neglecting the specifically religious features of Christianity in favor of the ethical, and by claiming to return to the "pure" sayings and parables of the "real" Jesus, presumably free from all later theological extrapolation (as if the sayings traditionally attributed to Jesus do not themselves contain a great deal about sin, judgment and salvation). And the reasons why Royce found this attempt unsatisfactory are not far to seek. He saw, first, that the classic Christianity of the New Testament communities, those fellowships to whom we owe whatever sayings and teachings of Jesus we now possess, maintained very definite views concerning sin and punishment, views which they believed to be in harmony with the spirit of Jesus; and, secondly, that any reinterpretation of Christianity which does not take these into account cannot be taken seriously as a statement of historical Christianity. Royce believed that the Christian view of man's sinful nature can be interpreted, and that in this respect it can be made intelligible to the modern mind, but he did not believe that the way to do this was to begin by denying most of what the Christian tradition has historically affirmed. What the early communities experienced, said Royce, must be taken, not as later and secondary additions to a previously given truth, but rather as a discovery of the further consequences and implications of the life and work of Jesus in relation to our common life. The beloved community as the locus of the divine spirit is, as it were, the guarantor of such further discoveries as were made. Applying this to the idea here in question, Royce pointed out that those early communities held views concerning sin and punishment, views which they believed to be the result of the divine spirit, that were based on ethical motives and possessed of an actual basis in human nature. It is on the basis of these considerations that Royce sought to interpret the idea of man's moral burden in an attempt to bridge the gap between the demands of the modern mind and the doctrines of classical Christianity.

No adequate account of Royce's view can be developed here,

but certain aspects, particularly those bearing on the theory of community, can be briefly considered. Every man, Royce said, knows, no matter how dimly or inadequately, what deed, if performed, would result in the forfeiting of his honor and integrity, all that he holds dear. This means that every moral agent[53] knows what consciously chosen deed would destroy the foundation of whatever moral code he recognizes. The having of an ideal which guides our conduct, and the knowledge of that deed for which we can "never forgive ourselves" are, according to Royce, correlative in the sense that to have one is at the same time to have the other. The having of an ideal requires as one of the conditions of its own existence as an expression of freedom, the possibility of the very betrayal of that ideal, and this betrayal is what is called, in religious language, sin. Royce said:

> To be aware of our coherent plan, to have a moral world and a business that, in ideal, extends to the very boundaries of this world, and to view one's life or any part of it, as an expression of one's own personal will, is to assert one's genuine freedom and is not to accept any external bondage. But it is also to bind one's self, in all the clearness of a calm resolve. It is to view certain at least abstractly possible deeds as moral catastrophes, as creators of chaos, as deeds whereby the self, if it chose them, would, at least in so far, banish itself from its own country.[54]

Sin, for Royce as well as for classical Christianity, means the *separation* of the sinner from the ideal which is both his guide in life (ethical) and that which gives his life meaning and purpose (religious). It was upon the consciously performed deed that betrays the ideal that Royce fixed his attention, and this deed, this *treason* against the ideal to which we are to be *loyal*, once performed, is irrevocable, according to Royce. What is meant by "irrevocable" is capable of precise statement; there never is a time when the proposition, "Such and such a deed of betrayal has been done by so and so" is false. This constitutes Royce's provocative and ingenious interpretation of what religious imag-

[53] It is well to note, in passing, the careful analysis by F. H. Bradley of the minimal conditions necessary for a "moral agent," in *Ethical Studies* (2nd ed.), pp. 3ff.

[54] *Ibid.*, I, 248.

ination has envisaged under the term "hell." Hell, on Royce's view, is the awareness on the part of the sinner and the community that the deed of betrayal is an irrevocable one, such that, although it may be transfigured in its meaning or changed in its consequences, it cannot be undone. This is the "hell of the irrevocable." In the light of such an idea it is easy to see why Matthew Arnold's advice to get rid of sin was, for Royce at least, if not in a certain obvious sense, nonsense, then, very close to it indeed. "For I am," said Royce, "and to the end of endless time shall remain, the doer of that wilfully traitorous deed."[55] The recognition of the fact that the traitorous deed leads to separation or alienation from the ideal, and also of the fact that such a deed is irrevocable in character leads at once to the problem of atonement: How can a man get rid of his sin and overcome the estrangement or "death" which is its inevitable consequence?

Atonement

In dealing with this third and last of the central Christian ideas, atonement,[56] Royce proceeded in his usual manner. He set for himself the tasks of interpreting atonement in purely human terms so that its experiential foundation would be made plain, and then of attempting to make the Christian idea of atonement intelligible to the modern mind making use of ideas developed in the completion of the first of these tasks. Curiously enough, since the idea of atonement has always been an enigma in the history of religion, Royce was more confident of success in his attempt to interpret this idea than in the case of any other. "The human aspect of the Christian idea of atonement," he said, "is based upon such motives, that if there were no Christianity and no Christians in the world, the idea of atonement would have to be invented, before the higher levels of our moral exist-

[55] *Ibid.*, I, 260f.

[56] The substance of Royce's view of this matter is to be found in *The Problem of Christianity*, I, Lects. VI and VII. The former chapter also appeared, with slight modifications, in *The Atlantic Monthly*, III (1913), pp. 406-409.

ence could be fairly understood.''[57] Yet despite this assurance at the outset, Royce's analysis is by no means easy to follow, nor is it entirely clear, and the question may legitimately be raised as to whether or no he has fixed his attention on certain features of atonement which have by no means been uppermost in classical Christianity. In considering his view, however, one must not overlook the fact that he deliberately confined his discussion to the bearing of atonement on the problem which resulted from the foregoing discussion of sin: How is the traitor to get rid of his sin? Consequently, it would perhaps be unreasonable to expect Royce's analysis to touch upon every phase of atonement as it appears both within and without Christianity.

The most important feature of atonement, on Royce's view, is the overcoming of estrangement suffered by the traitor[58] as the consequence of his treason. Atonement, therefore, if it is to be genuine, must reconcile the sinner both to himself and to the ideal world from which he has wilfully separated himself, and Royce is definite in his rejection of the view which holds that the sinner himself can and must perform the deed of atonement. He found this view unsatisfactory, first, because no deed the sinner can do can alter the fact that, from the sinner's own standpoint, he has done the deed for which he can ''never forgive himself,'' and, second, because, from the standpoint of the community, the irrevocable deed of the traitor, once committed, produces results which also cannot be undone and which pass far beyond the confines of the sinner's own experience. Hence the question naturally presents itself: Is there any event that can occur in the traitor's world which, while it cannot undo the evil deed, might yet enable the sinner to say, ''I am henceforth in some measure,

[57] This is the opening sentence from the first lecture on Atonement (*ibid.*, I, 271).

[58] Royce conceived the wilful sinner as one who has *betrayed* that which gives his life meaning and purpose. More precisely the necessary conditions for treason are:

i. The ideal must be the *cause* to which the person is devoted and which gives him meaning and purpose.

ii. One act of deliberate betrayal of the ideal must have been committed. See *The Problem of Christianity*, I, 278ff.

in some genuine fashion, morally reconciled to the fact that I did this evil?"[59] And further, can a deed occur which will not only lead the sinner to be thus reconciled to himself, but which will reconcile him to God as well? Christianity, as Royce was well aware, has always maintained that such an atoning event can occur in the sinner's world, although the nature and significance of that event has, for Christianity, been the subject of extended and often bitter controversy.

In the search for an adequate interpretation of atonement, Royce was led to consider, albeit briefly, both the classical *penal* theories of atonement and the more recent *moral* theories of the precise nature of Christ's work. It might be noted in passing that the distinctive characteristic of the penal theory is its emphasis upon the *objective* character of the process of atonement; it is something which takes place beyond the sinner's consciousness, despite the fact that the sinner must finally come to know that atonement has been accomplished and that he is "saved." The moral theories, on the other hand, have tended to stress the *subjective* aspect of atonement, focussing attention on the psychological state of the believer rather than upon some objective transaction beyond him. Royce, as will be seen, tried to save both these features, hence he found himself in agreement with neither one side nor the other as he understood these positions. No discussion of these theories in strictly theological terms was offered by Royce at all because he wished to approach the problem from an ethical and religious standpoint. He endeavored to view the matter as the sinner himself might view it, and not simply as it presents itself to a thinker interested in providing a theoretical answer to an exceedingly difficult question in theology. Hence, if the exponents of more strictly theological discussions of atonement find Royce's treatment inadequate, it is probably because they lose sight of what he called the "human" aspect of atonement. Unfortunately, no complete discussion even of Royce's own brief treatment of the problem can be given here, but only a statement of the salient features.[60]

[59] *Ibid.*, I, 281.

[60] Those books to which Royce was most indebted for his discussion of atone-

The penal theory, in so far as it involves an objective transaction, the *substitution* for the sinner of one who atones in order
to satisfy an angry God, was rejected as an adequate interpretation
of atonement by Royce largely on religious grounds. In his view,
such a theory fails because it cannot speak to the condition of the
sinner who, because he must be reconciled to himself as well as
to God, looks for something more than a theory maintaining that
another has been substituted or given as a ransom for his sin.
It is precisely in so far as the penal theory views atonement as
such an external transaction based on legal considerations, in
which the individual personality of the sinner does not enter,
that Royce found it unsatisfactory. Moberly expresses this very
well as follows:

> All forms of theory which are content to explain the Atonement as a
> transaction, however pathetic or august in itself, which has its proper
> completeness altogether outside the personality of the redeemed, are
> found to be hopelessly inadequate, as well to the truth of theological
> doctrine, as to the truth of human experience and reason.[61]

On the other hand, Royce found equally unsatisfactory the
moral theory of atonement proposed by Sabatier and other critics
of the penal or judicial interpretation. While the moral theory
does take account of the consciousness of the sinner[62] in a way
not envisaged by the penal interpretation, still this view was

---

ment are: Auguste Sabatier, *The Doctrine of Atonement*, 1904; R. C. Moberly, *Atonement and Personality*, 1901; and Percy Gardner, *The Religious Experience of St. Paul*,
1913. Sabatier, as is well known, severely criticized the penal theories of atonement as held by Irenaeus, Gregory of Nyssa, Ambrose and even Augustine, and
the satisfaction theory outlined in Anselm's *Cur Deus Homo*, while he attempted
to set forth a moral theory of atonement according to which the deed of Christ
evokes such repentance and love in the mind and heart of the sinner that this
leads to forgiveness. Royce was indebted to the analysis and historical data of
Sabatier although he could not accept his position. Compare *The Problem of
Christianity*, I, 288ff. with *The Doctrine of Atonement*, pp. 110ff. In the case of Moberly the situation is quite different. Royce found himself in substantial agreement
with Moberly's discussion. See *Atonement and Personality*, pp. 256ff., 277ff.

[61] R. C. Moberly, *Atonement and Personality*, p. 277.

[62] See *The Problem of Christianity*, I, 292, where Royce referred to the moral
theory as "true" but inadequate because it asks the sinner to do something which
he already has done and it does not suffice. (See below.)

not deemed sufficient by him because it counsels the sinner to do something—namely, to repent—which he not only has already done, but something the very doing of which constitutes his hell of remorse. "He has this repentance," Royce remarked, "as the very breath of what is now his moral existence in the hell of the irrevocable."[63] Repentance is not sufficient because it is already implied in remorse, the moral "hell" of the traitor. What neither repentance, good works, tears, or even love itself can effect is the changing of the irrevocable character of the traitorous deed, and, if, said Royce, reconciliation is to be achieved, some transfiguration of that deed's character as "irrevocable" must be effected. With this in mind, Royce turned from this view to a further possibility, one which he believed to be both an adequate interpretation of atonement and in harmony with classical Christianity.

It is at this point that the community begins to play an all-important role in Royce's discussion. The deed of the traitor, he said, is not only "private" in the sense that it is confined to the person of the doer alone, but it is "public" in that it breaks an objective bond of unity, that is, *sin destroys the community*. For if betrayal involves an ideal and an ideal a cause, then the traitor is one who, to a degree, destroys the community that has existed and been sustained by free allegiance to that cause. This "public" character of sin makes it necessary to shift the ground of the problem of atonement to that of the community. "The problem of reconciliation, then," said Royce, "—if reconciliation there is to be,—concerns not only the traitor, but the wounded or shattered community."[64] This means that the problem as previously stated: How can the traitor get rid of his sin? becomes: Can the beloved community in any way reconcile the sinner both to himself and to itself?

The community, as Royce was well aware, cannot solve the problem of atonement through either punishment or repentance alone, and the query may legitimately arise: Is there some new deed done either by, or on behalf of, the community which can

[63] *Ibid.*, I, 291.
[64] *Ibid.*, I, 294f.

lead to the required reconciliation? Royce believed such a deed is possible and the statement of the nature of that deed constitutes the nerve of his interpretation of atonement. The community as the spiritual unity of those loyal to the cause upon which it is founded needs an active and spontaneous loyalty and love if it is to be sustained. No mechanical allegiance will suffice. The truly beloved community is based on freedom and upon the faith and the constantly renewed choices of its members; above all, it is not made up of puppets. It is, however, precisely this basis in freedom that makes treachery or disloyalty to the community possible. "In a world where there is such free and good faith," said Royce, "there can be treason,"[65] and indeed the testimony of experience is that the more fervent and exalted the faith and the love, the deeper and more tragic the treason when it comes. Sin, then, is what destroys the bond of love uniting the community, and it is this above all else that constitutes the tragedy of the irrevocable for Royce. Atonement, if it is to be an actuality at all, must bring out of the tragedy of a broken community a new bond of love reconciling the traitor both to himself and to the ideal from which he has been estranged.

All of this, Royce constantly pointed out, appears again and again in the most obvious and familiar human experiences. He did not want his analysis to be taken solely as an exercise in theology in a narrow sense of the term. He sought to clarify what he called the human aspect of atonement, and he hoped to uncover the basis in human nature and experience of the traditional religious ideas he was considering. He expressed this clearly if somewhat too eloquently in the following passage concerning the problem of atonement:

That problem is daily faced by all those faithful lovers of wounded and shattered communities, who, going down into the depths of human sorrow, either as sufferers or as friends who would fain console, or who, standing by hearths whose fires burn no more, or loving their country through all the sorrows which traitors have inflicted upon her, or who, not weakly, but bravely grieving over the woe of the whole human world, are still steadily determined that no principality and no power,

[65] *Ibid.*, I, 299.

that no height and no depth, shall be able to separate man from his true love, which is the triumph of the spirit. That human problem of atonement is, I say daily faced, and faced by the noblest of mankind.[66]

To return to the main point of the discussion, Royce believed that there is a genuine triumph over treason and that such a triumph is made possible by the work of some suffering servant who at the same time embodies the spirit of the community itself.[67] Such a servant accomplishes, through some creative act, that reconciliation which is of the essence of atonement. What exactly is the nature of this creative deed? According to Royce, the work of the suffering servant is capable of precise analysis. First, the condition necessary for the atoning deed is some particular act of treason, and, secondly (and most important), the atoning deed must so transform the situation within which it occurs, that the result is a world that is better than it would have been had no deed of treason been done at all. This indeed, said Royce, can transform the meaning of the past in such a way that, while the past is not undone, it is no longer what it was either to the sinner or to the community, because that past has now become the necessary condition for a "new triumph of the spirit." "The traitor," said Royce, "cannot thus transform the meaning of his own past. But the suffering servant can thus transfigure this meaning; can bring out of the realm of death a new life that only this very death rendered possible."[68] What Royce was maintaining here can be expressed more precisely by saying that estrangement from the ideal (sin) is the necessary condition of reconciliation (atonement), and that while sin as sin is not literally undone, since this is impossible, it does not remain after the atoning deed what it had been before that deed was done.[69]

[66] *Ibid.*, I, 305.

[67] Royce said that the deed must be done "by or on behalf of" the community. Actually these are the same in so far as the suffering servant incarnates the spirit of the community. See *The Problem of Christianity*, I, 306ff.

[68] *Ibid.*, I, 309.

[69] See Athanasius, *De Incarn. Verbi.* 10; Irenaeus, *Against Heresies*, **Book III**, xix, xxiv; and esp. Gregory of Nyssa, *The Great Catechism*.

Royce was anxious to commend his interpretation as an "objective" account of atonement. That is, he did not want atonement to appear to be some purely "mental" transformation confined to the consciousness of the sinner alone. While he recognized, as has been shown, the primary importance of the change in the personality of the traitor wrought by atonement, he did not want to lose sight of what is accomplished in "public" terms with respect to the community, by the concrete deed of atonement. Consequently he stressed the idea that the creative deed results in the restoration of the broken community and this is indeed the state of affairs which is better than it would have been had no treason occurred in the first place. It is at this point that Royce turned to what he believed Christianity has always maintained about the life and work of Christ. He said:

Christian feeling, Christian art, Christian worship have been full of the sense that *somehow* (and *how* has remained indeed a mystery) there was something so precious about the work of Christ, something so divinely wise . . . about the plan of salvation,—that, as a result of all this, after Christ's work was done, the world as a whole was a nobler and richer and worthier creation than it would have been if Adam had not sinned.[70]

That Royce called attention to what has indeed been a genuine

[70] *Ibid.*, I, 319. Compare the following lines from a fifteenth-century Christian carol:

1. Adam lay ybounden
    Bounden in a bond;
   Four thousand winters
    Thought he not too long.

2. And all was for an apple,
    An apple that he took,
   As clerkes finden written
    In their book.

3. Ne had the apple taken been,
    The apple taken been,
   Ne had never our lady
    A-been heavene queen.

4. Blessed be the time
    That apple taken was.
   Therefore we moun singen
    Deo gracias!

Thomas Aquinas discussed the relation of sin to the work of Christ, but more specifically with respect to incarnation. He said that the work of incarnation was ordained by God as a remedy for sin, but that this does not mean that God could not have been incarnate were it not for sin. *Summa Theol.*, III. Qu. 1 art. 3.

part of Christian thought about atonement cannot be denied,[71] but it is seriously to be doubted whether this aspect of atonement has been uppermost in the minds of Christians when they have directed their attention to the meaning of the work of Christ. To say that atonement transfigures sin and achieves the desired reconciliation of the sinner is indeed to be faithful to Christianity; but to go further and say that atonement leads to a world which is better than it would have been if no sin had been committed in the first place, introduces a problem of theodicy which shifts the emphasis from the *overcoming* of sin to *explaining* its origin or *justifying* its necessity. Christianity has certainly held that the doctrine of atonement does, in some sense, answer the perplexing questions men have raised concerning the positive evil which is so much a part of human experience, and in so far as this is the case, atonement is not irrelevant to the traditional problems of evil. But Royce's emphasis tended so decidedly in the direction of making the essence of atonement consist in the justification of sin that his interpretation cannot easily be defended against the charge of its being one-sided.[72]

Recapitulation

Now that the three central Christian ideas, as Royce called them, have been briefly set forth, there remains the task of reviewing the relation in which the latter two, sin and atonement, stand to the first, the beloved community. That the community idea is central to Royce's general philosophical position and to his interpretation of Christianity is clear, but a study of the doctrine of community must attempt to provide as detailed an account of its nature and function as possible. Hence something

---

[71] There is no opportunity here for an extended historical discussion, but Athanasius, at least, may be mentioned as one who explicitly stressed that aspect of atonement which Royce developed. See *De. Incarn. Verbi.* 22. *Cf.* Moberly, *Atonement and Personality*, pp. 348-365. See also the lucid discussion of Aulèn in his *Christus Victor.*

[72] Full justice to Royce's interpretation has not, of course, been done here, but the nature of this study makes it impossible to discuss his interpretation of Christianity further.

further must be said about Royce's view of the beloved community in relation to the other parts of what Royce called the Christian "doctrine of life." Actually such a doctrine must embrace the ideas of the church, of sin and of atonement because for Royce a doctrine of life should provide us with "a connected survey of some notable portion of our duty, and an insight into the nature and source of the supreme values of our existence."[73] Such a synoptic view of life requires reference to man's situation and to his duty as well as to that redemption which is of the essence of high religion. The important thing is that, for Royce, a doctrine of life must be grounded upon the beloved community which is the proper locus of the divine spirit. Hence it is that he grouped the Christian ideas he has examined about the idea of the community or the church.

The Christian doctrine of life may be narrowed down so as to center about two concepts, the individual and the community.[74] The original sin of man consists in his isolation from the community, an isolation brought about by his own rebellion against the very community which first developed his self-consciousness.[75] Conscious sin is the outcome of such estrangement from the community and consists in wilful acts of disloyalty which not only threaten the existence of the community, but separate the sinner from the object of his devotion even further. This, said Royce, is the Christian view of the human situation, and he added, it is precisely because Christianity sees that man as sinner is unable of his own accord to throw off his "moral burden" that it is a religion of salvation and not simply an ethic or a set of rules

[73] *The Problem of Christianity*, I, 328.

[74] See *ibid.*, I, 343. Compare this with Royce's earlier interest in the "world and the individual." See also the informative remarks by Loewenberg on the continuity of Royce's thought in his introduction to *Fugitive Essays*, Cambridge, 1925.

[75] It should be noted here that Royce is closest to Hegel when he makes sin *necessary* as he seems to do. Sin is *necessary* as a condition of self-consciousness and it may be questioned as to whether sin can be both *necessary* and a result of the misuse of freedom. Niebuhr takes this as a paradox and likes to speak of sin as *inevitable* but not *necessary*, a distinction which needs to be understood in religious rather than theological terms. See *The Nature and Destiny of Man*, I, 251ff.; also Hegel's *Logic*, in the *Encyclopaedia* (Trans. Wallace), p. 24.

for living. As a religion of salvation, Christianity is a religion of loyalty to Royce, and consequently a religion centering about the community which redeems.

The individual soul in Christianity, said Royce, has an infinite significance in the sight of God because he is destined to be a member of the kingdom of heaven, and, on the other hand, the beloved community is the special object of God's concern because it is the body of the Christ and the instrument which redeems men from their inescapable burdens and from their naturally "lost" state. The individual and the beloved community are fundamental then, on Royce's view, because neither one can exist without the other. Fulness of life for individuals is not to be found apart from the beloved community. This community, nevertheless, is of the highest importance only in so far as it is the locus of the divine spirit which seeks to realize the redemption of all mankind. It is because Royce recognized the role of the beloved community as that which is destined to be the completed kingdom of heaven[76] that he rejected the interpretation of Christianity as simply a religion in which individuals are guided and inspired by one extraordinary individual (Jesus). This, according to Royce, would reduce Christianity to an ethic to the neglect of its decidedly religious emphasis upon redemption through incorporation into the Spirit of Christ, or in Paul's language, redemption through "putting on Christ." To Royce, to put on Christ is to be a member of that beloved community which is his body.

Ethically and religiously the beloved community in Christianity, the true locus of the Christ as continuing spirit, is at the center of the Christian doctrine of life. In religious terms, love for God is to be manifested by the individual as love for the Spirit of the Christ present as the unity of the community; in ethical terms, one's duty to show forth love to the neighbor is made concrete through the community because the "neighbor" is a member of that community along with oneself, and the one spirit serves to interpret all the neighbors to each other. Thus

[76] A careful study of Paul will show that Royce was justified in calling attention to this as Paul's own view of the matter.

love of God and love of neighbor, the two objects of the great Christian commandment, are translated into concrete terms for all individuals through that community which is truly the body of Christ.

Royce, as is now apparent, was aware however that the ideal as stated is "not yet," and that a true doctrine of life based on the actual situation of mankind must not fail to take into account the positive and the destructive powers of sin, moral evil, ignorance and pain. Consequently such a doctrine of life must do more than speak of love to God and more than command love of neighbor; it must also provide for the redemption of men from the original sin of their social contentiousness and from the unbearable burden of their wilful acts of treason. Such redemption requires a deed or deeds which are atoning, that is, which overcome the original sin of social contentiousness by establishing that divine community capable of training the self without leading him to conscious rebellion, and also which transform the irrevocable deeds of conscious treason by bringing out of them such triumph in restoring community as would not otherwise have been possible. Thus atonement enters to complete the Christian doctrine of life, for the work of atonement is what continually preserves the beloved community despite the destructiveness of sin and of moral evil.

The "problem of Christianity" which consists, according to Royce, in the mediation of the central affirmations of Christianity to the modern mind, can be solved through the understanding (in so far as the acceptance of Christianity is a problem of *understanding*) of both the theory and the reality of the beloved community. On Royce's view, when the proper relation between the individual and the community, together with the relation between the Christ and his community, is understood, Christianity's doctrine of life embracing both a way of life and a process of redemption will no longer appear to the modern mind as outworn, but rather as an adequate comprehension of man's nature and of his ultimate destiny.

CHAPTER SIX

THE GREAT COMMUNITY

In his last years, those just preceding the first World War and the American entry into that struggle, Royce came to state his views concerning man's ideal by reference to what he called the "Great Community." Hence it seems wise, in attempting to set forth the contribution of the community idea to Royce's thought, to outline his view of this community and at the same time touch briefly upon his scheme for a community of insurance, a scheme which he believed might well be influential in making the international or great community a present reality. The most significant aspect of the great community is that it is *international* in scope, and that all men beyond the divisions of nation, race and class are destined to be among its members. Royce in attempting to analyze the moral issues posed by the war, rejected the view that would make the conflict a struggle between the opposed interests of individual nations alone, in favor of the view that looks upon the war as "a conflict between the community of mankind and the particular interests of individual nations."[1] On such a view, no single nation in any conflict can ever be right in its cause unless that cause is the community of all mankind, the great community. This community has to do with the unified interests of humanity, and precisely because these interests cannot be confined by the distinctions of nation or of race, they must represent the cause of the truly universal community. The guiding and unifying spirit of this community was, for Royce, the same spirit which he took to be at the basis of the beloved community, the *caritas* or charity of which St. Paul so vividly spoke. Royce's understanding of this Christian virtue was both broad and profound and he never tired of pointing out new domains to which it is relevant. Concerning charity,

[1] *The Hope of the Great Community*, p. 31.

162

and the type of relation between persons it makes possible, he said:

It is a virtue which Paul recommends to his Corinthians as to an united community who, in the bonds of the spirit, are one body despite the multitude of the members. Charity never faileth, and outlasts all earthly vicissitudes in its own heavenly world, because there we know even as we are known, and our mutual relations are those of a perfected spiritual community.[2]

One of the greatest tragedies of human history, and it is never more evident than in time of a war involving many nations, is that men of different nations and races are forced to enter into relations with each other, both because of their common conflicts and their common interests, before the great community with its cause and its ideal of charity has an opportunity to show itself. Men stand under the necessity, a necessity which becomes more insistent as the world grows closer together, of entering into relations of all kinds long before the common cause of all men becomes conscious and is understood. Until such a cause, the common interests of all men, is recognized and made the object of free and conscious devotion, mankind will continue to dwell together, but they will do so without true community and the spirit of charity which must accompany this. It was primarily with this tragedy and all its consequences that Royce was concerned when he directed attention to the great community. For, he believed, only in a community devoted to the cause of all mankind in its myriad interests and filled with the spirit of charity are such relations between men established that self-realization and fulfillment pass from the sphere of ideality to that of concrete reality.

Royce's stress on the importance of the community as all-embracing totality must not lead one to think that he considered the members of no moment, for he hastened to point out that, while ethical individualism has often been the foe of the community because of its emphasis on purely personal happiness or virtue, ethical collectivism is "equally useless, for the attainment

[2] *Ibid.*, pp. 34f.

of humanity's great end."[3] And the reason for his rejection of collectivism, which he associated with Bentham's utilitarianism and the idea that community is only a collection is that it speaks not about the great community but about aggregates designated as the "greatest number." Such aggregates were scarcely adequate for Royce because, involving no cause and no spirit or interpreter, and without a common memory and a common hope, they lack what is essential for true community. Yet it must be borne in mind that despite the stress on the community as a real being, Royce never lost sight of those who make it up, for, as he pointed out on many occasions, there are no communities without members. Applying this directly to the great community it means that, on Royce's view, the individual nations and all the lesser communities within them are not to be annihilated in some gigantic world state. He said, concerning this highly important consideration:

Therefore, while the great community of the future will unquestionably be international by virtue of the ties which will bind its various nationalities together, it will find no place for that sort of internationalism which despises the individual variety of nations ... whatever that form of loyalty which is now patriotism expresses, must be in spirit preserved by the great community of the future.[4]

One of the most interesting features of this final interpretation of loyalty developed by Royce is that he relied not on the political, but on the social and cultural activities and interests of men as the means of calling attention to the international cause and of bringing about the great community. Royce was not of the opinion that political problems are the most important in such an enterprise, and he even struck a prophetic note when he suggested that there is a real opposition between the possession by one nation of great political powers and that nation's making a contribution to the ideal goods of the great community.[5] The judicial and commercial enterprises of men were the really significant

---

[3] *Ibid.*, p. 43.

[4] *Ibid.*, p. 50.

[5] *Ibid.*, p. 57.

cant and fruitful ones to Royce, and it was upon these that he based his hopes for the realization of the great community. How seriously he took this can be seen in that very interesting, even if somewhat bizarre, part of his thought: the idea that insurance in its various forms could be a means of establishing and extending community on an international scale.

In his small but highly significant volume entitled *War and Insurance*, Royce set out to deal with the problems of world community and in particular with the further application of his theory of the community of interpretation to these problems. He took off from some reflections of Kant concerning the relation between social antagonism and social development contained in the latter's essay of 1784, "The Idea of a Universal History."[6] In that writing Kant had spoken of the function of social antagonism in effecting the development of man's latent powers, and he had even gone so far as to render thanks to nature "for the insatiable thirst after wealth and power!"[7] to be found in all human beings. Royce was much impressed by this analysis because his whole idea of establishing community of various sorts involved the overcoming of certain inevitable chasms, division, antagonisms and strife through the reconciling function of interpretation. While Kant was attempting to explain the "unsocial sociality" of man as a device employed by "the adjusting hand of a wise creator" for the perfecting of man's potentialities, Royce was interested in stressing the vital importance of finding ways to reconcile and overcome such social strife through the creation of community.

Royce pointed out that, whereas Hobbes had stressed the "war of all against all" on the one hand, and Rousseau had proclaimed that men by nature would live in harmony were it not for the distortions of culture on the other, Kant saw deeper than both. Kant, according to Royce, held that men both love

[6] An English translation attributed to Thomas de Quincey appeared in *The London Magazine*, Oct. 1824. This translation was reprinted by The Sociological Press, Hanover, N.H., 1927.

[7] *The Idea of a Universal History* (Hanover, N.H.: The Sociological Press, 1927), p. 6.

and hate each other and that one impulse feeds the other. He said: "Kant's formula for the natural relations of a pair of human beings is that the natural man can 'neither suffer his fellow nor do without him.' "[8]

Royce took Kant's view to mean that by nature any two men always constitute what, in Royce's language, is to be called a "dangerous pair." Two men together, even or especially those who love each other, will naturally conflict with each other and become a potential source of strife. Such relations Royce called dyadic or dual and he regarded them as the source of evil and contention, inevitably leading to social confusion and disaster. "When mutual friction," said Royce, "once arises between a pair of lovers or of rivals or of individuals otherwise interestingly related . . . *the friction tends to increase.*"[9]

The dangerous or dyadic relations are not confined to individuals in society, on Royce's view, but they represent as well the most prevalent cause of war and international strife. Nations are almost always related chiefly in pairs, pairs of borrowers, lenders, traders, etc.; and from these dangerous relations arise the suspicions and conflicts that lead to war and to the destruction of whatever basis for genuine community ever exists. What is required, Royce thought, both in the most purely personal relations and in the most complex and far-reaching relations between national states, is the transformation of the dangerous or dyadic relations into communities or triadic relations with the resulting reconciliation made possible by the "thirds" or interpreters. Royce outlined several important types of such communities in the political and social part of his thought, but it was to the possibility of a community of insurance that he looked as a means of eliminating war and of establishing the great community.[10]

[8] *War and Insurance*, p. 29.

[9] *Ibid.*, p. 35.

[10] Since a complete and adequate treatment of the insurance community is beyond this study, it should be pointed out that Royce's theory will certainly be misunderstood if it is taken simply as a utopian scheme. He had worked out the details of the insurance community carefully and had consulted experts in the field (see *War and Insurance*, pp. iv–v.). At least one of the *prima facie* arguments in favor of the practicability of his view is that it does not require the

Royce viewed insurance as a business having a unifying and reconciling function. The forms of insurance exemplify what he called the community of insurance, a community of interpretation possessing the same triadic structure characteristic of community of whatever sort. The triadic structure of the community of insurance is clear; the interpreter mediates between the interests of two persons whose concerns, being in some fundamental sense in conflict, need to be reconciled or interpreted one to the other. The insurance corporation functions as just such an interpreter. The insurance principle may be best illustrated by the instance of life insurance. Here Royce called the opposed or conflicting interests those of the "adventurer" and the "beneficiary," and he viewed these two as an illustration of what he called a "dangerous pair" of human beings; dangerous because their conflicting interests might lead to such wrongs and divisions as would ultimately be destructive of community.[11] Since the basic danger, as has been shown, of having people related by a dual or dyadic relation is that tensions and possible upheavals always result from such situations, precisely no community of understanding is possible between persons when there are only two, that is, when, in logical terms, the relation is *dyadic*. Royce's solution, and it is easy to see from this how seriously he regarded the idea of interpretation, was to bring these dangerous pairs into community as follows:

A. Adventurer   B. Beneficiary

C. Insurance Corporation

A and B constitute the "dangerous pair" and C is the interpreter.

Royce believed that the insurance community ("mutual inter-

---

setting up of a great deal of administrative machinery not now in existence. On the contrary the community of insurance is a present reality. Royce believed it could be greatly extended to perform a reconciling function not hitherto recognized and exploited.

[11] *The Hope of the Great Community*, pp. 62ff. Cf. *War and Insurance*, pp. 28ff.

national insurance'') is not necessarily to be confined to the
relations between individuals but that it might be extended to
perform a novel and highly significant function in promoting
the cause of world peace through becoming international in scope.
This belief led him to formulate the principles of his plan for a
world insurance body, or board of trustees. He urged, in the
tragic days preceding America's entry into the first World War,
that the method of insurance was one which had not yet been
tried in the interests of promoting peace among nations. *"Apply,"*
he said, *"to international relations, gradually and progressively, the
principle of insurance which has been found so unexpectedly fruitful
and peaceful and powerful and unifying in the life and in the social
relations of individual men."* [12]

Royce worked out his plan with precision and in detail, but
the details are not the concern of this study. What is of significance for an understanding of his community theme is recognition
of the fact that the insurance community functions as a community of interpretation with its reconciling function and its
concern for linking together many selves in one common cause,
just as the other communities of interpretation do. In all of them
it is the reconciling function of the interpreter or "third" that
performs the task of uniting the members and preserving the
community, as a passage like the following makes clear—

... in each of these communities, one of the members has the essentially
spiritual function or task of representing or interpreting the plans, or
purposes, or ideas, of one of his two fellows to the other of these two
in such wise that the member of the community whom I call the "interpreter" works to the end that these three shall cooperate as if they
were one, shall be so linked that they shall become members one of
another, and that the community of the whole shall prosper and be
preserved. [13]

The spirit of loyalty is the foundation of the insurance community just as surely as it supports the other communities of
which Royce spoke. Loyalty had for him an absolutely basic

---

[12] *War and Insurance*, pp. 66f.
[13] *The Hope of the Great Community*, p. 64.

importance and it was capable of being expressed in many ways all of which lead to the founding of some particular community. Such community provided an admirable solution to his deepest ethical problems because it includes not only individual self-realization through the carrying out of some concrete duty, but it unites persons beyond divisive tensions and conflicts in a common loyalty to a cause which transcends them all.

BIBLIOGRAPHY

(The following bibliography represents addenda to the bibliography of Benjamin Rand to be found in *Papers in Honor of Josiah Royce*, 1916, pp. 287-94. This volume appeared as Vol. XXV, No. 3, May, 1916 of *The Philosophical Review*.)

A. *PRIMARY WORKS*

1. BOOKS

The Hope of the Great Community. New York, 1916.
Lectures on Modern Idealism. New Haven, 1919.
Fugitive Essays. Introd. by Dr. J. Loewenberg, Cambridge, Mass., 1920.

2. ARTICLES

The Concept of the Infinite. *Hibbert Journal*, Vol. I (1902), pp. 21-45.
An Extension of the Algebra of Logic. *Journal of Philosophy*, Vol. X. (1913), pp. 617-33.
Charles Sanders Peirce (with F. Kernan). *Journal of Philosophy*, Vol. XIII. (1916), pp. 701-9.
Nietzsche. *Atlantic*, Vol. 119 (1917), pp. 321-31.

B. *SECONDARY WORKS*

1. BOOKS

Aronson, M. J., *La philosophie morale de Josiah Royce*. Paris, 1927.
Barrett, C., Editor, *Contemporary Idealism in America*. New York, 1920.
Dykhuizen, George, *The Conception of God in the Philosophy of Josiah Royce*. Chicago, 1936.
Galgano, M., *Il pensiero filosofico e morale di Josiah Royce*. Rome, 1921.
Iakovenko, B., *L'idealisme costruttivo ed assoluto di Josiah Royce*. Praga, 1937.
Leidecker, K. F., *Josiah Royce and Indian Thought*. New York, 1931.
Marcel, Gabriel, *La metaphysique de Royce*. Paris, 1945.

Perry, Ralph Barton, *In the Spirit of William James*. New Haven, 1938.

Philp, J. H., *The Principle of Individuation in the Philosophy of Josiah Royce*. New Haven, 1916.

Rothman, W., *Josiah Royce's Versuch einer Synthese von Pragmatismus und Objectivität*. Jena, 1926.

Santayana, G., *Character and Opinion in the United States*. New York, 1920.

Townsend, H. G., *Philosophical Ideas in the United States*. New York, 1934.

2. Articles and Notices

Bakewell, C. M. "True Philosopher," *Nation*, Vol. 103 (1916), pp. 461-63.

Bixler, J. S., "Josiah Royce—Twenty Years After," *Harvard Theological Review*, Vol. XXIX (1936), pp. 197-224.

Bronstein, D. J., "Royce's Philosophic Method," *Philosophical Review*, Vol. XLIII (1934), pp. 471-82.

Chapman, J. J., "Portrait of Josiah Royce, the Philosopher," *Outlook*, Vol. 122 (1919), p. 372.

Cohen, Morris R., "Philosophy of Josiah Royce," *New Republic*, Vol. 18 (1916), pp. 264-66.

—— "On American Philosophy; the Idealistic Tradition and Josiah Royce," *New Republic*, Vol. 20 (1919), pp. 148-50.

Dewey, John, "Reply to Professor Royce's Critique of Instrumentalism," *Philosophical Review*, Vol. XXI (1912), pp. 69-81.

Dykhuizen, G., "Royce's Early Philosophy of Religion," *Journal of Religion*, Vol. XV (1935), pp. 316-21.

Hook, S., "Our Philosophers," *Current History*, Vol. 41 (1935), pp. 698-704.

Jacks, L. P., "Collective Security," *Hibbert Journal*, Vol. 34 (1936), pp. 172-77.

Jefferson, H. B., "Royce on the Problem of Evil," *Journal of Religion*, Vol. XI (1931), pp. 359-77.

Johnson, P. E., "Josiah Royce: Theist or Pantheist?" *Harvard Theological Review*, Vol. XXI (1928), pp. 197-205.

—— "The Religious Philosophy of Josiah Royce," *Hibbert Journal*, Vol. 33 (1935), pp. 375-84.

Mead, G. H., "The Philosophies of Royce, James, and Dewey in their American Setting," *International Journal of Ethics*, Vol. XL (1930), pp. 211-31.

Monsman, P., "Royce's Conception of Experience and of the Self," *Philosophical Review*, Vol. XLIX (1940), pp. 325-45.

Portrait, *Scientific Monthly*, Vol. 30 (1930), p. 118.

Portrait, *Time*, Vol. 27 (1936), p. 13.

Ramsey, P., "The Idealistic View of Moral Evil: Josiah Royce and Bernard Bosanquet," *Philosophy and Phenomenological Research*, Vol. VI (1945-46), pp. 554-89.

Slattery, C. L., "Josiah Royce," *Outlook*, Vol. 121 (1919), pp. 114-5.

Sorley, W. R., "Josiah Royce, 1855-1916," *Proceedings of the British Academy*, 1915-16, pp. 585-92.

Townsend, H. G., "The Pragmatism of Peirce and Hegel," *Philosophical Review*, Vol. XXXVIII (1928), pp. 297-303.

INDEX

Absolute, 12ff., 16ff., 32ff., 119, 126

Actual infinite ("social infinite"), 8n, 11, 14, 26n, 31ff., 40, 63, 85, 107

Albright, W. F., 68n

Amos, 61, 100n

Anselm, 152n

Aquinas, St. Thomas, 115n, 157n

Arnold, M., 145, 150

Athanasius, St., 156n, 158n

Atonement, 124f., 133, 150ff.

Augustine, St., 136n, 152n

Aulèn, G., 158n

Barrett, C., 19n

Bergson, H., 6, 66, 78f., 95f., 98

Boas, G., 107n

Balzano, B., 32

Bosanquet, B., 32

Bradley, F. H., 12n, 31f., 41n, 51, 113n, 136n, 137n, 149n

Brown, W. A., 119f.

Calkins, M., 68n, 107n

Calvin, J., 129

Cantor, G., 32

Carr, E. S., 109n

Cohen, M. R., 94n

Community, 4, 7ff., 19, 26ff., 74ff.
    beloved, 10, 123ff., 127ff.
    great, 3, 162ff.
    insurance, 3, 166ff.
    scientific, 4ff., 9, 28, 30

Community of interpretation, 6ff.. 106ff., 166ff.

Conscience, 143

Cornill, C. H., 103n

Darwin, C., 99f.

Dedekind, R., 20n, 32, 89

De Morgan, A., 21, 23f., 31, 91ff.

Dewey, J., 18n, 37n, 43, 46n, 48, 105

Error, 12ff., 18, 19

Fundamentalism, 133

Gardner, P., 152n

God, 67, 83n, 89, 110f., 114, 129f., 135ff., 146, 152, 160f.

Gregory of Nyssa, 152n, 156n

Harnack, A., 109n, 133n

Hegel, 12n, 20, 32, 38n, 41n, 78n, 85n, 104, 119, 159n

Hobbes, 165

Hocking, W. E., 8n, 73, 119f., 122

Hosea, 61

Hume, 75n

Individualism, 65, 132n, 142ff.

Induction, 28f.

Interpretant ("third"), 20ff., 92

Interpretation, 5ff., 22ff., 78ff., 116
    function of comparison in, 20ff., 92ff.
    relation of perception and conception to, 78ff., 97ff.
    time process and, 82ff.

Interpreter, 7, 10, 13, 22, 85, 99, 105, 111ff., 166ff.

Intuition, 24ff., 69ff., 96

Isaiah, 100ff.

Jacks, L. P., 96ff., 141

James, W., 47ff., 64ff., 78, 110

Jesus Christ, 115ff., 127, 133ff., 145ff., 152, 157, 160

Kant, 9, 12, 18, 27, 37, 41, 53n, 78, 81, 118n, 165ff.

Kierkegaard, S., 136

Loewenberg, J., 3, 86ff., 159n

Loyalty, 9, 35ff., 52ff., 132, 168f.
    love and, 76, 138ff.
    truth and, 47ff., 53ff.

Luther, M., 124, 127

175